The
Original
World Wide Web

Written & Illustrated
by B. K. Hixson

The Original World Wide Web

Copyright © 2003
First Printing • August 2003
B. K. Hixson

Published by Loose in the Lab, Inc.
9462 South 560 West
Sandy, Utah 84070

www.looseinthelab.com

Library of Congress Cataloging-in-Publication Data:

Hixson, B. K.
        The Original World Wide Web/B. K. Hixson
        p.   cm.-(Loose in the Lab Science Series)

        Includes index
        ISBN 1-931801-07-X
    1. Ecology experiments-juvenile literature. [1. Ecol-
ogy experiments 2. Experiments] I. B. K. Hixson
II. Loose in the Lab III. Title IV. Series
QP37.H24   2003
612

Printed in the United States of America
The Silent Spring roars!

Dedication

Tribe Evans of Redlands

This book is for my nieces and nephews who share a knowledge and love of the land that is derived from their heritage of two cultures. As Navajo, your ancestors lived on and had an intimate relationship with the land for hundreds of years. It is hard not to imagine that that connection with the land, an appreciation and respect for its ways, and an innate understanding of its significance in our lives is not deeply ingrained in your souls.

On the other hand, you come from a long line of good cowboy stock that lives on today. And as anybody who has spent long hours in the saddle on the back of a horse can tell you, there is plenty of opportunity to take in the beauty of the land, learn Ma Nature's house rules, and understand firsthand the roles of predator and prey, both as observer and participant.

Many happy years traveling this beautiful planet,

Bryce

Acknowledgments

Scouting exposed me to nature and encouraged me to appreciate it. Growing up in Western Oregon, where the rain and rich volcanic soil provides an abundance of plant and animal life, I was privileged to spend my weekends running through the forest, trampling the wildflowers, and providing coronaries for small mammals as I played Capture the Flag, Kick the Can, and a variety of tracking games, and as I foraged for something dry to build a fire with each evening. Despite my decadently youthful ways, I learned about ecosystems, biomes, plant and animal habitats, food webs, food chains, and native species, to the extent that I decided to put my capitalist tendencies aside and spend an entire summer as the Nature Area Counselor on the backside of Mt. Hood, sharing this knowledge with other Scouts. Back in 1973, I think my entire paycheck for 8 weeks was $72.00 and all the camp-food I could stomach, but the experience was worth a million.

As for my educational outlook, the hands-on perspective, and the use of humor in the classroom, Dr. Fox, my senior professor at Oregon State University, gets the credit for shaping my educational philosophy while simultaneously recognizing that, even at the collegiate level, we were onto something a little different. He did his very best to encourage, nurture, and support me while I was getting basketloads of opposition for being willing to swim upstream. There were also several colleagues who helped to channel my enthusiasm during those early, formative years of teaching: Dick Bishop, Dick Hinton, Dee Strange, Connie Ridgway, and Linda Zimmermann. Thanks for your patience, friendship, and support.

Next up are all the folks who get to do the dirty work that makes the final publication look so polished but very rarely get the credit they deserve. Our resident graphics guru, Kris Barton, gets a nod for scanning and cleaning the artwork you find on these pages, as well as putting together the graphics that make up the cover. A warm Yankee yahoo to Eve Laubner, our editor, who passes her comments on so that Kathleen Hixson and Eve Laubner (once again) can take turns simultaneously proofreading the text while mocking my writing skills.

Once we have a finished product, it has to be printed so that Gary Facente, Louisa Walker, Lisa Lachance, and the Delta Education gang can market and ship the books and collect the money.

Mom and Dad, as always, get the end credits. Thanks for the education, encouragement, and love. And for Kathy and the kids—Porter, Shelby, Courtney, and Aubrey—hugs and kisses.

Repro Rights

There is very little about this book that is truly formal, but at the insistence of our wise and esteemed counsel, let us declare: *No part of this book may be reproduced or utilized in any form or by any means, electronic or mechanical, including photocopying, recording, or by any information storage and retrieval system, without permission in writing from the publisher.* That's us.

More Legal Stuff

Official disclaimer for you aspiring scientists and lab groupies: This is a hands-on science book. By the very intent of its design, you will be directed to use common, non-toxic household items in a safe and responsible manner to avoid injury to yourself and others who are present while you are pursuing your quest for knowledge and enlightenment in the world of ecology. Just make sure that you have a fire blanket handy and a wall-mounted video camera to corroborate your story.

If, for some reason, perhaps even beyond your own control, you have an affinity for disaster, we wish you well. *But we in no way take any responsibility for any injury that is incurred to any person using the information provided in this book or for any damage to personal property or effects that is directly or indirectly a result of the suggested activities contained herein.* Translation: You're on your own, despite the fact that many have preceded you in the lab.

Less Formal Legal Stuff

If you happen to be a home schooler or very enthusiastic school teacher, please feel free to make copies of this book for your classroom or personal family use—one copy per student, up to 35 students. If you would like to use an experiment from this book for a presentation to your faculty or school district, we would be happy to oblige. Just give us a whistle and we will send you a release for the particular lab activity you wish to use. Please contact us at the address below. Thanks.

Special Requests
Loose in the Lab, Inc.
9462 South 560 West
Sandy, Utah 84070

Table of Contents

The National Content Standards (K–4)

• *All animals depend on plants. Some animals eat plants for food. Other animals eat animals that eat plants.*

• *An organism's pattern of behavior is related to the nature of that organism's environment, including the kinds and numbers of other organisms present, the availability of food and resources, and the physical characteristics of the environment. When the environment changes, some plants and animals survive and reproduce, and others die or move to new locations.*

• *Humans depend on their natural and constructed environments. Humans change environments in ways that can be either beneficial or detrimental for themselves and for other organisms.*

The National Content Standards (5–8)

• *A population consists of all individuals of a species that occur together at a given place and time. All populations living together and the physical factors with which they interact compose an ecosystem.*

• *Populations of organisms can be categorized by the functions they serve in an ecosystem. Plants and some microorganisms are producers—they make their own food. All animals, including humans, are consumers that obtain food by eating other organisms. Decomposers, primarily bacteria and fungi, are consumers that use waste materials and dead organisms for food. Food webs identify the relationships among producers, consumers, and decomposers in an ecosystem.*

• *For ecosystems, the major source of energy is sunlight. Energy entering ecosystems as sunlight is transferred by producers into chemical energy through photosynthesis. That energy then passes from organism to organism in food webs.*

The 6 Big Ideas about Nature

Big Idea 1 • There are many relationships in the natural world. Some exist between two individual species; others involve a large, complex web of associations.

Big Idea 2 • Many cycles exist in nature. These cycles allow for the use and renewal of natural resources, such as air, water, soil, and nutrients.

Table of Contents

Big Idea 6 • Pollution adversely affects our environment and the ability of plants and animals to live and thrive in their particular ecosystems.

Who Are You ? And ...

First of all, we may have an emergency at hand and we'll want to cut to the chase and get the patient into the cardiac unit, if necessary. So, before we go too much further, **define yourself**. Please check one and only one choice listed below and then immediately follow the directions that appear *in italics*. Thank you in advance for your cooperation.

I am holding this book because ...

___ **A. I am a responsible, but panicked, parent.** My son / daughter / triplets (circle one) just informed me that his / her / their science fair project is due tomorrow. This is the only therapy I could afford on such short notice. This means that, if I were not holding this book, my hands would be encircling the soon-to-be-worm-bait's neck.

Directions: Can't say this is the first or the last time we heard that one. Hang in there; we can do this.

1. Quickly read the Table of Contents with the worm bait. The Big Ideas define what each section is about. Obviously, the kid is not passionate about science, or you would not be in this situation. See if you can find an idea that causes some portion of an eyelid or facial muscle to twitch.

If that does not work, we recommend narrowing the list to the following labs because they are fast, use materials that can be acquired with limited notice, and their intrinsic level of interest is generally quite high.

How to Use This Book

2. Take the materials list from the lab write-up and from page 179 of the Science Fair Project section and go shopping.

3. Assemble the materials and perform the lab at least once. Gather as much data as you can.

4. Go to page 179 and read the materials list. Then start on Step 1 of Preparing Your Science Fair Project. With any luck, you can dodge an academic disaster.

____ **B. I am worm bait.** My science fair project is due tomorrow, and there is not anything moldy in the fridge. I need a big Band-Aid, in a hurry.

Directions: Same as Option A. You can decide if and when you want to clue your folks in on your current dilemma.

____ **C. I am the parent of a student who informed me that he/she has been assigned a science fair project due in six to eight weeks.** My son/daughter has expressed an interest in science books with humorous illustrations that attempt to explain ecology and associated phenomena.

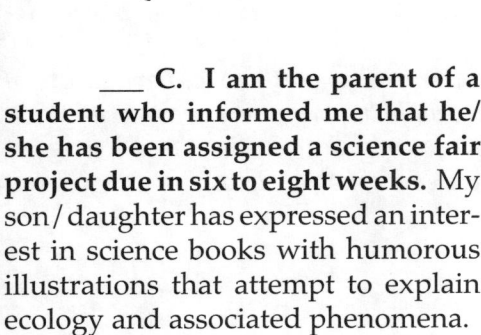

Who Are You ? And ...

Directions: Well, you came to the right place. Give your kid these directions and stand back.

1. The first step is to read through the Table of Contents and see if anything grabs your interest. Read through several experiments, see if the science teacher has any of the more difficult-to-acquire materials, like dissecting materials, spreading boards, plant presses, and some of the chemicals, and ask if they can be borrowed. Play with the experiments and see which one really tickles your fancy.

2. After you have found and conducted an experiment that you like, take a peek at the Science Fair Ideas and see if you would like to investigate one of those or create an idea of your own. The guidelines for those are listed in the Science Fair section. You have plenty of time, so you can fiddle and fool with the original experiment and its derivations several times. Work until you have an original question you want to answer, and then start the process. You are well on your way to an excellent grade.

___ **D. I am a responsible student and have been assigned a science fair project due in six to eight weeks.** I am interested in ecology, and despite demonstrating maturity and wisdom well beyond the scope of my peers, I too still have a sense of humor. Enlighten and entertain me.

Directions: Cool. Being teachers, we have heard reports of this kind of thing happening, but usually in an obscure and hard-to-locate town, several states removed. Nonetheless, congratulations.

Same as Option C. You have plenty of time and should be able to score very well. We'll keep our eyes peeled when the Nobel Prizes are announced in a couple of decades.

How to Use This Book

___ **E. I am a parent who home schools my child/children.** I am always on the lookout for high-quality curriculum materials that are not only educationally sound but also kid- and teacher-friendly. I am not particularly strong in science, but I realize it is a very important topic. How is this book going to help me out?

Directions: In a lot of ways, we created this book specifically for home schoolers.

1. We have taken the National Content Standards, the guidelines that are used by all public and private schools nationwide to establish their curriculum base, and listed them in the Table of Contents. You now know where you stand with respect to the national standards.

2. We then break these standards down and list the major ideas that you should want your kid to know. We call these the Big Ideas. Some people call them objectives, others call them curriculum standards, educational benchmarks, or assessment norms. Same apple, different name. The bottom line is that when your children are done studying this unit on ecology, you want them not only to understand and explain each of the Big Ideas listed in this book, but also, to be able to defend and argue their positions based on experiential evidence that they have collected.

3. Building on the Big Ideas, we have collected and rewritten 50 hands-on science labs. Each one has been specifically selected so that it supports the Big Idea that it is correlated to. This is critical. As the kids do the science experiment, they see, smell, touch, and hear the experiment. They will store that information in several places in their brains. When it comes time to comprehend the Big Idea, the concrete hands-on experiences provide the foundation for building the Idea, which is quite often abstract.

Who Are You ? And ...

*For example: I can show you a recipe in a book for chocolate chip cookies and ask you to reiterate it. Or I can turn you loose in a kitchen, have you mix the ingredients, grease the pan, plop the dough on the cookie sheet, slide everything into the oven, and wait impatiently until they pop out eight minutes later. Chances are that the description given by the person who actually made the cookies is going to be much clearer because it is based on a true understanding of the process, **because it is based on experience.***

4. Once you have completed the experiment, there are a number of extension ideas under the Science Fair Extensions that allow you to spend as much or as little time on the ideas as you deem necessary.

5. A word about humor. Science is not usually known for being funny, even though Bill Nye, The Science Guy, *Beaker from* Sesame Street, *and* Beakman's World *do their best to mingle the two. That's all fine and dandy, but we want you to know that we incorporate humor because it is scientifically (and educationally) sound to do so. Plus it's really at the root of our personalities. Here's what we know:*

When we laugh ...
a. Our pupils dilate, increasing the amount of light entering the eye.
b. Our heart rate increases, which pumps more blood to the brain.
c. Oxygen-rich blood to the brain means the brain is able to collect, process, and store more information. Big I.E.: increased comprehension.
d. Laughter relaxes muscles, which can be involuntarily tense if a student is uncomfortable or fearful of an academic topic.
e. Laughter stimulates the immune system, which will ultimately translate into overall health and fewer kids who say they are sick of science.
f. Socially, it provides an acceptable pause in the academic routine, which then gives the student time to regroup and prepare to address some of the more difficult ideas with a renewed spirit. They can study longer and focus on ideas more efficiently.
g. Laughter releases chemicals in the brain that are associated with pleasure and joy.

6. If you follow the book in the order in which it is written, you will be able to build ideas and concepts in a logical and sequential pattern. But that is by no means necessary. For a complete set of guidelines on our ideas on how to teach home-schooled kids science, check out our book, Why's the Cat on Fire? How to Excel at Teaching Science to Your Home-Schooled Kids.

How to Use This Book

___ F. I am a public/private school teacher, and this looks like an interesting book to add ideas to my classroom lesson plans.

Directions: It is, and please feel free to do so. However, while this is a great classroom resource for kids, may we also recommend several other titles: Survival of the Fittest *(Adaptation),* Chains, Webs, and Other Associations *(Food Webs and Food Chains),* Cycling Around the Planet *(All Six of the Major Cycles),* Take Note *(Techniques for Studying, Collecting, and Preserving Plants and Animals in the Wild), and* Peeing in the Pool *(Pollution and Its Effects on the Environment).*

These books have teacher-preparation pages, student-response sheets or lab pages, lesson plans, bulletin board ideas, discovery center ideas, vocabulary sheets, unit pretests, unit exams, lab practical exams, and student grading sheets—basically everything you need if you are a science nincompoop, and a couple of cool ideas if you are a seasoned veteran with an established curriculum. All of the ideas that are covered in this one book are covered much more thoroughly in the others that we listed. They were specifically written for teachers.

___ G. My son/daughter/grandson/niece/father-in-law is interested in science, and this looks like fun.

Directions: Congratulations on your selection. Hook them up with a pass to the local science museum and you've got the perfect Saturday afternoon gig.

___ H. I have this incredible temptation to forage in the wild, nibble on plants, and lay lots of eggs. Any ideas?

Directions: Probably a flashback to an entomology class. Feel free to forage; that's healthy. If you have any luck with the eggs, call us and we'll see if we can get you booked on an afternoon TV show.

Lab Safety

Contained herein are 50 science activities to help you better understand the nature and characteristics of ecology as we currently understand these things. However, because you are on your own in this journey, we thought it prudent to share some basic wisdom and experience in the safety department.

Read the Instructions

This is an interesting concept, especially if you are a teenager. Take a minute before you jump in and get going to read all of the instructions, as well as the warnings. If you do not understand something, stop and ask an adult for help.

Clean Up All Messes

Keep your lab area clean. It will make it easier to put everything away at the end and may also prevent contamination and the subsequent germination of a species of mutant tomato bug larvae. You will also find that chemicals perform with more predictability if they are not poisoned with foreign molecules.

Organize

Translation: Put it back where you get it. If you need any more clarification, there is an opening at the landfill for you.

Dispose of Poisons Properly

This will not be much of a problem with the labs that are suggested in this book. However, if you happen to wander over into one of the many disciplines that incorporates the use of advanced chemicals, then we would suggest that you use great caution with the materials and definitely dispose of any and all poisons properly.

Practice Good Fire Safety

If there is a fire in the room, notify an adult immediately. If an adult is not in the room and the fire is manageable, smother the outbreak with a fire blanket or use a fire extinguisher. When the fire is contained, immediately send someone to find an adult. If, for any reason, you happen to catch on fire, **REMEMBER: Stop, Drop, and Roll.** Never run; it adds oxygen to the fire, making it burn faster, and it also scares the bat guano out of the neighbors when they see the neighbor kids running down the block, doing an imitation of a campfire marshmallow without the stick.

Protect Your Skin

It is a good idea to always wear protective gloves whenever you are working with chemicals. Again, this particular book does not suggest or incorporate hazardous chemicals in its lab activities. If you do happen to spill a chemical on your skin, notify an adult immediately and then flush the area with water for 15 minutes. It's unlikely, but if irritation develops, have your parents or another responsible adult look at it. If it appears to be of concern, contact a physician. Take any information that you have about the chemical with you.

Lab Safety

Save Your Nose Hairs

Sounds like a cause celebre L.A. style, but it is really good advice. To smell a chemical to identify it, hold the open container six to ten inches down and away from your nose. Make a clockwise circular motion with your hand over the opening of the container, "wafting" some of the fumes toward your nose. This will allow you to safely smell some of the fumes, without exposing yourself to a large dose of anything noxious. This technique may help prevent a nosebleed or your lungs from accidentally getting burned by chemicals.

Wear Goggles If Appropriate

If the lab asks you to heat or mix chemicals, be sure to wear protective eyewear. Also have an eyewash station or running water available. You never know when something is going to splatter, splash, or react unexpectedly. It is better to look like a nerd and be prepared than to schedule a trip down to pick out a Seeing Eye™ dog. If you do happen to accidentally get chemicals into your eye, flush the area for 15 minutes. If any irritation or pain develops, immediately go see a doctor.

Lose the Comedy Routine

You should have plenty of time scheduled during your day to mess around, but science lab is not one of them. Horseplay breaks glassware, spills chemicals, and creates unnecessary messes—things that parents do not appreciate. Trust us on this one.

No Eating

Do not eat while performing a lab. Putting your food in the lab area contaminates your food and the experiment. This makes for bad science and worse indigestion. Avoid poisoning yourself and goobering up your labware by observing this rule.

Happy and safe experimenting!

Recommended Materials Suppliers

For every lesson in this book, we offer a list of materials. Many of these are very easy to acquire, and if you do not have them in your home already, you will be able to find them at the local grocery or hardware store. For items that are more difficult to acquire, we have selected for your convenience a small but respectable list of suppliers who will meet your needs in a timely and economical manner. Call for a catalog or quote on the item that you are looking for, and they will be happy to give you a hand.

Loose in the Lab
9462 South 560 West
Sandy, UT 84070
Phone 1-888-403-1189
Fax 1-801-568-9586
www.looseinthelab.com

Delta Education
80 NW Boulevard
Nashua, NH 03063
Phone 1-800-442-5444
Fax 1-800-282-9560
www.delta-education.com

Nasco
901 Jonesville Avenue
Fort Atkinson, WI 53538
Phone 1-414-563-2446
Fax 1-920-563-8296
www.nascofa.com

Ward's Scientific
5100 W. Henrietta Road
Rochester, NY 14692
Phone 1-800-387-7822
Fax 1-716-334-6174
www.wardsci.com

Educational Innovations
151 River Road
Cos Cob, CT 06807
Phone 1-888-912-7474
Fax 1-203-629-2739
www.teachersource.com

Frey Scientific
100 Paragon Parkway
Mansfield, OH 44903
Phone 1-800-225-FREY
Fax 1-419-589-1546
www.freyscientific.com

Fisher Scientific
485 S. Frontage Rd.
Burr Ridge, IL 60521
Phone 1-800-955-1177
Fax 1-800-955-0740
www.fisheredu.com

Sargent Welch Scientific Co.
911 Commerce Ct.
Buffalo Grove, IL 60089
Phone 1-800-727-4368
Fax 1-800-676-2540
www.sargentwelch.com

The Ideas, Lab Activities, & Science Fair Extensions

Big Idea 1

There are many relationships in the natural world. Some exist between two individual species; others involve a large, complex web of associations.

Food Chain Relationships

The Experiment

We are going to start off this section on interdependent relationships right in the middle of the pigpile, with food chains. This is a generic term that can be used in any ecosystem or biome to show the relationships between the different plants and animals in that system.

Because it is a generic term, we are going to introduce you to a model rather than to specific relationships between plants and animals. You can get to specifics when you study your local flora and fauna. What you are interested in finding out with this lab is who eats whom and the relationship between different levels in a food chain.

Materials

13 Food chain cards, quarter sheet of paper
    1 Tertiary (3°) consumer
    2 Secondary (2°) consumer
    4 Primary (1°) consumer
    6 Producers
1 Wire hanger
1 Roll of tape
1 Box of crayons

Procedure

1. Do some research on your geographic region and find out which animals and plants are native to your area. The best place to start is the Web, but your library may have good information also.

You are going to build a model of a food chain for your local area on a wire hanger and display it.

2. To build your specific food chain, you are going to need to start at the bottom, with the producers. These are the plants in your area. They take sunlight, gas from the atmosphere, water, and nutrients, and combine them to form plant matter, which is the food for the primary consumers. Pick 6 local plants and draw and label 6 of your food chain cards.

3. Next up are the primary consumers. These are either insects or herbivores (animals that eat plants only). Select four animals that like to snack on plants. Draw, color, and label the cards for those animals.

4. Secondary consumers are animals that eat other animals that eat plants. For example, a bug (primary consumer) eats the leaf of a plant (producer). The bug, in turn, is eaten by a toad (secondary consumer). Select two secondary consumers, draw, color, label, and set those cards aside for later.

5. Finally, select one tertiary consumer. In our example, that would be a snake that eats the toad that eats the bug that is snacking on the plant. (There has got to be a song like that somewhere.)

6. Place your coat hanger on the table and arrange rows of food chain cards so that they represent the levels of the food chain. Tape them in place, and display them when you are done.

If you would rather just build a generic model of a food chain with generic descriptions, we have included four food chain cards on the next page. You may copy and use them. It's up to you.

Food Chain Relationships

Producer

1° Consumer

2° Consumer

3° Consumer

Data & Observations

List the producers and consumers from your local area that you chose in order to make the model.

A. Producers (plants)
1. _____
2. _____
3. _____
4. _____
5. _____
6. _____

B. Primary consumers (insects/herbivores)
1. _____
2. _____
3. _____
4. _____

C. Secondary consumers (insects/reptiles/amphibians)
1. _____
2. _____

D. Tertiary consumers (animals)
1. _____

How Come, Huh?

By laying out the food chain, you can start to get a feel for the different relationships between plants and animals. The interdependence is a little more sophisticated than we have represented here, but we will develop it further in later labs.

Symbiotic Circle

The Experiment

Symbiosis is a term that describes a mutually beneficial relationship between two species. One of the most notable examples of symbiosis exists with lichen. In this case, the symbiosis occurs when an alga and a fungus work together. The fungus provides the structure (the house, if you will) that the alga lives in. The alga, in return, collects sunlight and produces food for the fungus. They live together harmoniously.

This experiment takes off on that idea. You will need 15 to 20 of your friends or family members to help you out. You and all of these people are going to form a symbiotic circle where everyone in the circle is going to be able to sit down and at the same time provide a seat for someone else.

Materials

15-20 Friends (all about the same size)
1   Grassy area

Procedure

1. Ask everyone who is helping you to stand in a close, tight circle. This activity usually works better if you have one person act as the supervisor, standing on the outside of the circle, directing people to their places.

2. The circle should be very tight and as round as possible. Once the circle is formed, ask each person to place her hands on the shoulders of the person in front of her. Be sure to keep all elbows out to the side and feet at a shoulder width apart.

3. This is the fun part. On the count of three, everyone in the circle sits down at the same time. As each person sits, her legs will bend and form a seat for the person in front of her. If you do this slowly and all at one time, each friend will be able to sit on the lap of the person behind her, while providing a seat for the person in front of her. Hence, this is a symbiotic circle.

How Come, Huh?

The idea behind doing this lab is to illustrate the interdependence of things in a food chain, food web, ecosystem, or biome. The ability of each organism to be successful is directly dependent on the organism with which it is most closely associated.

Science Fair Extensions

1. Take a peek at lichens and how they function symbiotically. There are many different kinds of lichens in lots of cool colors, such as fluorescent green, orange, and yellow. They typically grow on rocks and are a very important part of creating soil.

Food Webs

The Experiment

Rachel Carson's book, *Silent Spring*, pointed out that we are not independent of our environment. All things are interconnected and influence one another. By dumping DDT into the environment to remove insects, we inadvertently poisoned animals up the food chain.

This activity is designed to demonstrate the interdependence of all things and the effect that eliminating one portion of the web has on all of its other components.

Materials

1   Set of food web cards
1   Ball of yarn
1   Squirt bottle with water
15-20 Friends

Procedure

1. Make a set of food web cards. (For purposes of specificity, each card has a picture of a Texas plant or animal.) Attach a piece of yarn to each card so the card can be worn around the neck as a necklace. Use the ideas on the following pages or, if you would like, make a set that is unique to your environment.

2. Have your friends sit in a circle with the food web cards around their necks. They should all hold their right index fingers out like hooks.

3. Start by wrapping the yarn around the finger of the kid who is the sun. For our purposes, life starts here. Choose who should be next in the web, walk over to that person, and hook the yarn around that person's finger. Do not tie the yarn. The web must be flexible and must accommodate change. For example, the sun a) could connect to the plant and give it energy to make food, b) could evaporate the water, moving it along the water cycle, or c)  warm the frog that needs its energy and warmth to survive. As you can see, each step of the way has numerous options.

4. Continue connecting the web around the circle until everyone has been woven into the web at least once. Now spray DDT (i.e., water from the squirt bottle) on the insect. The DDT, of course, is going to kill the insect. The "insect" then straightens out her finger, releasing the yarn, and is no longer part of the food web. This leaves a hole in the food web. All of the other parts of the food web have to adapt and adjust.

5. Discuss the results. Notice that because all of the bugs are dead, the frogs, suffering from malnutrition, kick the bucket as well. (Have the frogs let go of the yarn.)

Try to figure out how the story might continue.

Food Webs

Eagle

Rattlesnake

Horned Lizard

Armadillo

Javelina

Red Spotted Toad

Brown Bat

White Tailed Deer

Food Webs

San Marcos Salamander

Swainson's Hawk

Coyote

Live Oak

Pinyon Pine

Mesquite

Food Webs

Creosote Bush

Texas Bluebonnet

Buffalo Grass

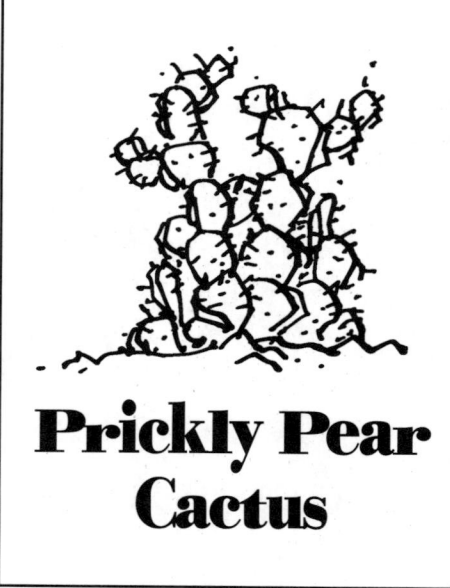

Prickly Pear Cactus

Mosquito

Sun

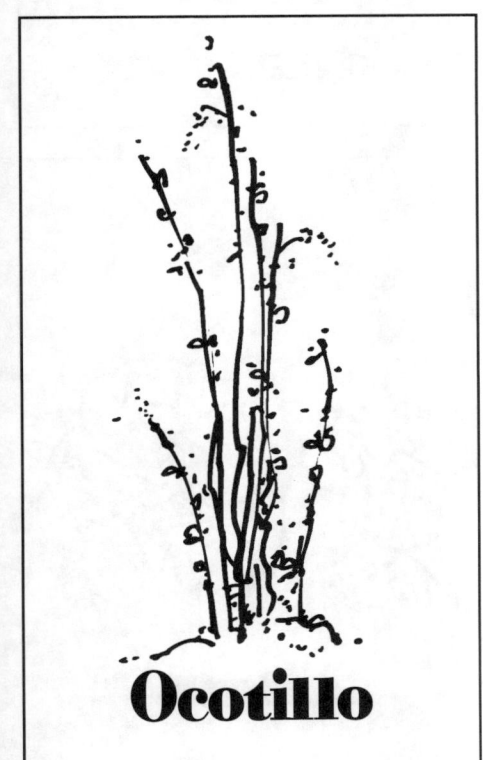

Ocotillo

Yucca

Food Webs

Humming-bird

Road Runner

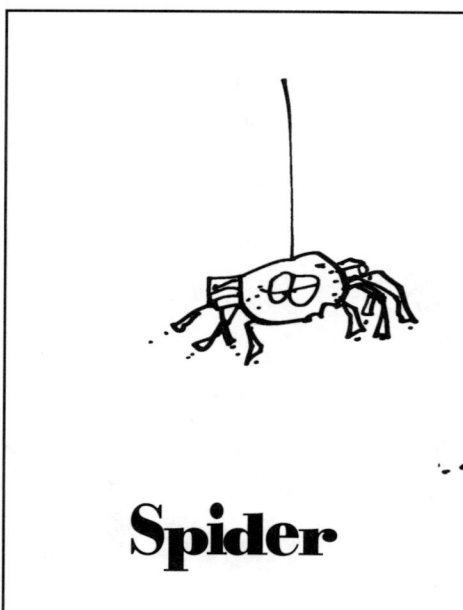

Spider

Horse

How Come, Huh?

Every time a species is removed from an ecosystem, the other plants and animals have to work to pick up the "slack" that is created by its absence. This is the same dilemma that is created in nature when large numbers of a single species are removed from an ecosystem. When that type of animal or plant dies, it not only reduces the numbers on the inventory sheet, but it may also jeopardize the survival of another species in the same ecosystem.

Science Fair Extensions

2. Develop a food web that is specific to your area. Pick local plants and animals. One of the best places to start is on the Net at the site for your state's wildlife agency. The agency will have tons of pictures, lists, and places you can visit to see the plants and animals that are indigenous to your area.

3. Create a standing model of an ecosystem, based on this model. Figure out a way to substitute for people so that you can use this model with small groups as well as large ones.

Owl Pellet Boneyard

The Experiment

Owls are at the top of the food chain as tertiary consumers. They eat snakes, mice, some insects, and small mammals that may happen to wander out onto the buffet table at night. Once owls catch their prey, they return to their roost (usually a large limb on a big tree) and they eat the catch of the day. If the prey is a large animal, such as a rabbit or a skunk, the owls will tear the meat from the bones. If it is a small meal, such as a mouse, vole, or snake, they will eat the animal whole.

Owls are not designed to digest bones and fur, so their stomachs take these indigestible materials, pack them into a pill shape, and the owl regurgitates the newly compacted package out onto the ground below its roost.

Your job today is to take an owl pellet, dissect it, and determine what the owl had for dinner.

Materials

1   Owl pellet
1   Pair of rubber gloves
1   Dissecting tray or paper plate
1   Pair of tweezers
1   Dissecting probe or toothpick
1   Pencil

Procedure

1. Owl pellets typically come packaged in a piece of tin foil. They are usually the size of an adult thumb. With your gloves on, remove the foil and set the owl pellet on the dissecting tray or paper plate.

2. Using the tweezers and the dissecting probe, gently tease the mat of hair and bones apart. (This is not an owl "poop," which is white and runny like most bird poop. Instead, it is compact bones, hair, and other materials that are not easily digested by the owl.)

3. As you pick through the pellet, you will find tiny skeletons, teeth and jaw sections, lots of matted hair, and bones from legs, arms, and feet. Separate the parts of the pellet and draw a picture of the bones that you have collected in the spaces that are provided.

4. When you have completed your dissection of the owl pellet, go online or head to the local library and find several pictures of mice, shrews, voles, and other animals that owls like to dine on. Compare the drawings that you have made or the actual bones if you have kept them, and identify as many of the bones as possible.

Data & Observations

1. In the space below, draw the animal skulls and teeth that you find in your owl pellet.

Owl Pellet Boneyard

2. In the space below, draw the animal leg and arm bones that you find in your owl pellet.

3. In the space below, draw any other goodies that you find in your owl pellet.

How Come, Huh?

This is an excellent way to learn exactly what an owl eats. The dinner bell rings, the meal is plucked from the high grass under the live oak, and it's taken to the big limb on the pinyon pine for dinner. We may not see the whole process, but by looking at the bones and reconstructing the animals that are found in the owl pellets, we can come to some very accurate conclusions about the eating habits of specific predators.

Science Fair Extensions

4. Do your very best to reassemble one of the skeletons so that it is intact. Given that the mouse, shrew, or vole was complete when it went down the gullet of the owl, it is a reasonable expectation that the entire skeleton, or at least most of it, can be found in the pellet.

5. Go on a roost hunt. Owls roost in trees, typically on large limbs. There are several clues to finding an owl roost. Look for the feces (the whitish-brown excrement that the owl will drop.) Look near the bases of large trees. You will also want to look for the presence of feathers and large animal parts, such as the skeletons of skunks or rabbits.

When you find a tree that appears to be a roost for an owl, start looking for the gray-brown pellets. Owls will regurgitate them near the base of the tree.

Aquarium Ecosystem

The Experiment

Another way to look at relationships between plants and animals is to observe them directly. The next two labs allow you to do that on land and in water.

First up is going to be a water environment. These are very easy to set up. (Most major chain stores and all pet shops will have a ready-to-go starter setup for an aquarium.)

Materials

1   Aquarium (10 gallons is a good size to start with)
1   Pump/filter
1   Bag of gravel or sand
1   Assortment of fish
1   Can of fish food
1   Bag of snails
     Chemicals to balance pH
     Plants
     Water

Procedure

1. Rinse the aquarium out with clean water and set it on a stable, level surface.

2. Cover the bottom of the aquarium with gravel or sand. Add stones, coral, or other widgets for fish to swim through, under, and around.

3. Place the pump/air filter in one corner of the aquarium. Be sure to run the air hose under the sand.

4. Fill the aquarium with water. Following the instructions in your kit, either balance the pH chemically, add dechlorination tablets, or let the water sit for 24 hours in direct sunlight.

5. Put the plants in the gravel, positioning them where you would like them.

6. Add the snails or other mollusks that will eat the algae and plankton that will naturally bloom inside your tank.

7. Finally, add your fish. To do so, place the closed bag inside the aquarium and allow the two water temperatures to become equal. Then, release the fish into the aquarium.

8. Feed, observe, and enjoy your fish.

FISH

SNAILS

PLANTS

WATER

GRAVEL

AQUARIUM

Aquarium Ecosystem

How Come, Huh?

The aquarium represents a mini-ecosystem. Although you introduce the food into the system for the fish, the fish are dependent on the plants for a renewed supply of oxygen, and the plants thrive on the carbon dioxide produced by the animals. The snails eat the algae and plankton that are produced in the water. The sun adds energy to the system. So, in many ways, this mini-ecosystem mirrors the larger systems of ponds and lakes.

Science Fair Extensions

6. Keep a log of activity, growth, life, and death in your aquarium. Monitor and record the following:

>   a. Growth of fish.
>   b. Growth of plant life.
>   c. Death of fish or plants.
>   d. Additional fish or mollusks that occur.
>   e. Color of water.
>   f. Amount of food eaten by fish.
>   g. Temperature of water.
>   h. Other ideas you may have.

7. Find out what is necessary to build, stock, and maintain a salt water aquarium.

Ecosystem in a Bottle

The Experiment

Terrariums are very nice to have, but they are expensive and require more time and money to maintain than this particular lab requires. Instead, in the place of a terrarium, you are going to take an ordinary 2-liter bottle and turn it into a mini-terrestrial ecosystem.

Materials

1   2-liter pop bottle w/end-cap
1   Pair of scissors
1   Pie tin
1   Quart of potting soil
1   Package of pea seeds
    Water
    Hot water
    Assorted bugs

Procedure

1. Hold the bottom of the 2-liter pop bottle under hot running water until the glue holding the end-cap on dissolves and allows the cap to come loose.

CUT HERE.

2-LITER
POP BOTTLE

2. Remove the cap from the bottom of the bottle and fill it with potting soil. Place the cap that is full of potting soil in the center of the pie tin.

3. Using a pair of scissors, cut the top of the bottle off. Use the illustration above as a guide, cutting across the dotted line. Toss the top of the bottle into the garbage can.

Ecosystem in a Bottle

4. Open the package of seeds. (We like peas because they grow quickly, they have cool-looking curly tendrils, and they'll provide you with something to eat when you are all done.)

Plant the peas in the soil. (You'll find that 6 to 10 peas fill a container nicely.) Water the peas.

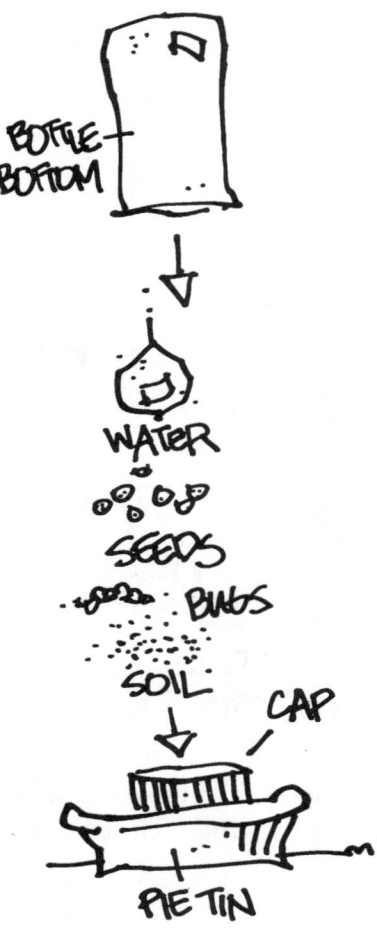

BOTTLE BOTTOM

WATER

SEEDS

BUGS

SOIL

CAP

PIE TIN

5. Head outside and flip over rocks and old boards, and peek in the corners of your garden for millipedes, worms, and any other invertebrates that you can find. Plunk them into the soil in your bottle bottom.

6. Flip the main plastic part of the bottle upside down and wiggle it into the end-cap. You now have an enclosed terrarium. To add water, which should not be necessary very often, simply pour it into the pie tin and let it get absorbed.

7. Make a journal and record the activity of the bugs, the appearance of water in the bottle, and the sprouting and growth of the peas.

Data & Observations

Using the space at the right, draw a picture of your ecosystem after one month.

How Come, Huh?

When you placed the bottle over the end-cap, you were creating a closed system. Nothing could get in, and nothing could get out. The sun still provided heat energy, which evaporated the water, but the water condensed on the surface of the bottle and ran back down into the soil.

The seeds and bugs exchanged gases, excrement, nutrients, and occasional jokes to provide the necessary components for a self-contained ecosystem.

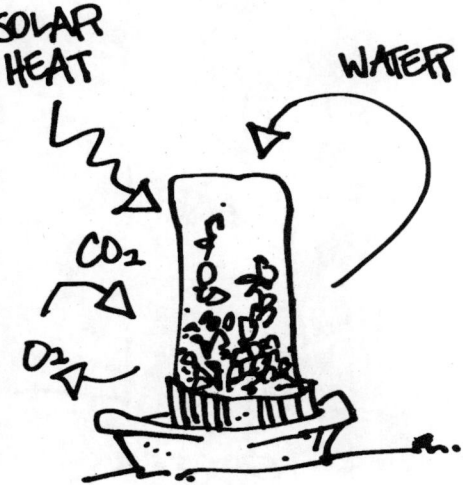

Science Fair Extensions

8. Super-size this experiment and use an aquarium. Your ecosystem can also be constructed in a 5-gallon water bottle. Both an aquarium and a bottle make impressive displays.

Cactus Garden

The Experiment

This lab takes a look at plants in a specific type of ecosystem, the desert, and does not focus so much on the relationship between plants, animals, and other components of an ecosystem.

Cactus gardens are interesting, require relatively low maintenance, and provide a peek at an environment that not everyone gets a chance to visit.

Materials

1   Shoebox
1   Plastic garbage can liner
1   Roll of tape
1   Bag of sandy soil
1   Pencil
    Variety of cactus plants
    Water

Procedure

1.   Place the garbage can liner inside the shoebox and tape it down so that it is secure.

2.   Fill the box with sandy soil and mix in a small amount of water.

3.   Add several cactus plants to the soil. They have extensive root systems, so be sure to give them lots of room to expand.

4.   Place the box in a warm, sunny spot.

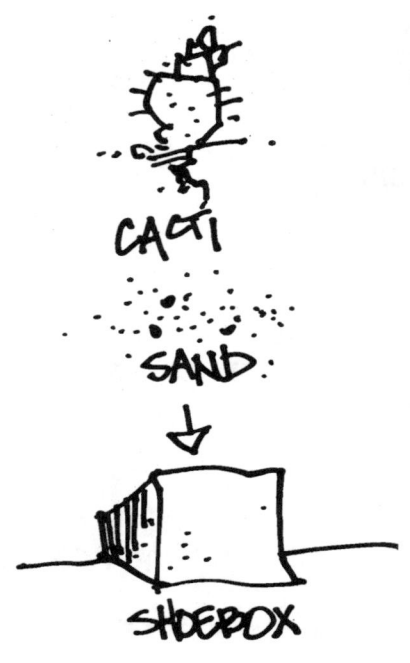

CACTI

SAND

SHOEBOX

How Come, Huh?

A desert, by definition, is a geographic region that receives less than 10 inches of rain per year over a period of 10 consecutive years. This means that water is sparse, and when it does rain, it usually comes in the form of downpours associated with thunderheads.

Because of these conditions, cacti have evolved to the point of having special adaptations that allow them to survive in this environment. They must collect water when it is available, store it for long periods of time, and prevent water loss whenever possible. To do all this, they have a waxy coating on the stem that prevents water loss, and they have leaves that are reduced to being needles. The center of the cactus is full of pulpy tissue that expands when water is available, and the root system is very extensive, sometimes running 100 feet or more from the base of the cactus.

Science Fair Extensions

9. If you live in or near a desert, head out into the wilds and look for cactus "skeletons" of teddy bear cholla and silver and golden cholla. These will give you clues about how the cactus survives in this environment.

10. Research the adaptations of other desert plants, such as the ocotillo, which produces leaves only after it rains, and the creosote bush, which produces a stinky, waxy secretion to prevent bugs from nibbling on its leaves.

Worm Composter

The Experiment

We are definitely going underground with this next lab. You
are not going to actually decompose worms, as the title would suggest, but you are going to create an
environment ideal for the decom-
position of other organic matter,
and this will be done with the assis-
tance of worms.

This is the last lab in this
section and, as a general rule, the
fungi, bacteria, and animals that
participate in garbage removal generally don't get as much credit as
they are due. Without this portion of the cycle, we would be up to our
eyeballs in dead carcasses, leaves, and matted grass, not to mention all
the feces that would be lying around. Decomposers are critical for
taking the refuse and putting it back into the system in a usable and
efficient form.

Materials

1   Shoebox with lid
1   Plastic garbage can liner
1   Roll of tape
1   Bag of potting soil
1   Carton of earthworms
     Assorted organic remnants
     Water

Procedure

1. Place the garbage can liner inside the shoebox and tape it
down so that it is secure.

2. Fill the box with potting soil and mix in the assorted organic remnants. Things that work well are potato peelings, apple cores, orange peels, leftover pasta, rice, and chunks of fat that has been trimmed off a steak.

3. Once you have mixed all the organic matter thoroughly, add a cup of water and mix that around. Finally, add the worms.

4. Cover the shoebox and place it in a warm, dark place. Observe what happens over time to the organic matter that you added, and also take stock of your worm population.

How Come, Huh?

The worms work their way through the soil and organic matter, and they actually "eat" both. The worms process this matter and then produce castings, which are high in mineral content and enrich the soil, making it more fertile.

Worms also produce holes in the soil, and this aerates it and provides oxygen to the roots of plants and to other animals that live underground. Working in combination with bacteria and other microorganisms, worms create a healthy ecosystem.

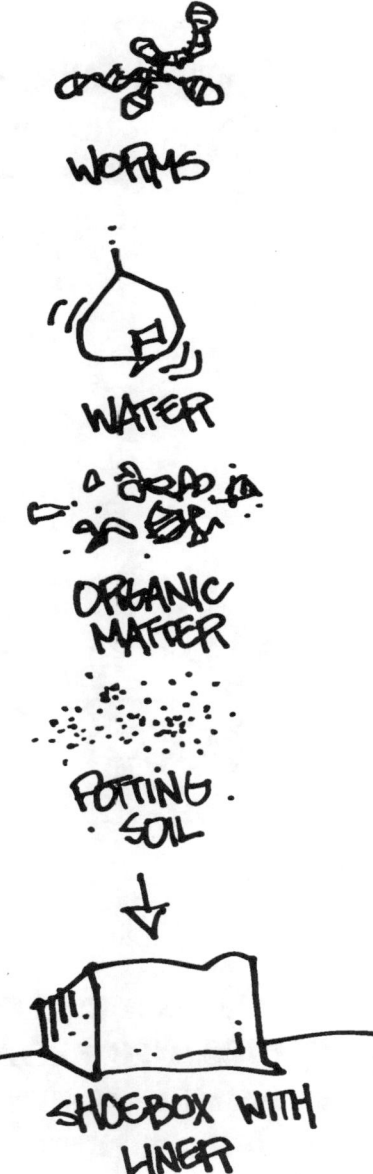

WORMS

WATER

ORGANIC MATTER

POTTING SOIL

SHOEBOX WITH LINER

Big Idea 2

Many cycles exist in nature. These cycles allow for the use and renewal of natural resources, such as air, water, soil, and nutrients.

Seasons

The Experiment

If you live on Earth, and presumably you do, and if you also happen to live in North America, you experience seasons to some degree. This lab explores the one simple reason for the seasons—the tilt of the Earth on its axis. As you will see, it is this tilt, coupled with the revolution of the Earth around the sun, that accounts for the coming and going of summer, autumn, winter, and spring.

Seasons are also responsible for triggering many of the changes that we see in ecosystems. These changes include foliage coming and going, the production of flowers and seeds, the birth of young animals, and the migration of others. Seasons are critical to ecosystem health and function.

Materials

1   High-intensity lamp
1   Large table
1   Globe on axis
1   Protractor
2   Liquid crystal thermometers
1   Meterstick
1   Pen or pencil
1   Roll of masking tape

Seasons

Procedure

1. Place the meterstick in the middle of a large table. Place a 2-inch strip of masking tape at either end of the meterstick. Rotate the meterstick 90 degrees and place two more 2-inch strips of tape at either end. You should have four strips of tape, equidistant from the center of the meterstick. Remove the meterstick and place a fifth piece of tape to mark the center position.

2. On the piece of tape closest to your belly button, write the word *summer*. The next piece of tape to the right is to be labeled *autumn*. Then label *winter* directly across from *summer*. Finally, label *spring*.

3. Place the high-intensity lamp on the fifth piece of tape in the middle of the table, pointing toward the piece of tape that says *summer*. Adjust the lamp so that it is shining directly across the table. Use the illustration on the previous page to help you set this up.

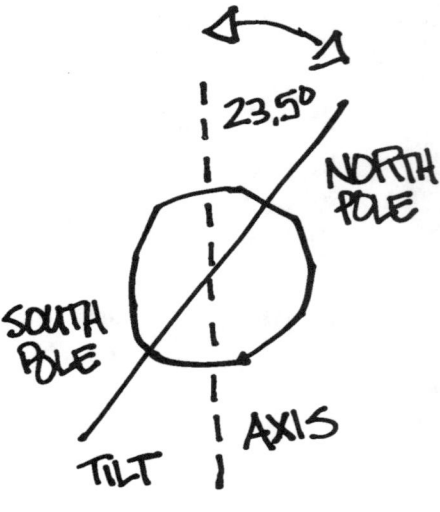

4. Using the globe with the adjustable axis and the protractor, check the tilt of the Earth and make sure that it is 23.5 degrees off-center. Use the illustration at the right as a guide.

5. Place the properly tilted globe on the piece of tape that says *summer*. Rotate the globe so that North America is closest to the sun, and tape one of the liquid crystal thermometers on the 30 degree latitude. Tape the other thermometer the same distance below the Equator, across Argentina and Chile.

The Original World Wide Web • B. K. Hixson

6. Allow the globe to be heated by the lamp for five minutes, and then record the temperature in the data table below. Then move the globe to *spring*, rotate the lamp so that it is shining directly on the Earth, and rotate the globe, keeping the tilt at 23.5 degrees. Shine the lamp on the two LC thermometers for five minutes. Record the temperatures.

7. Continue to rotate the lamp and globe through the other two seasons, recording the temperature each time. When you are done, compare the temperatures with the seasons and see if they follow the natural pattern of changes that we have here on Earth.

Data & Observations

Season	Temp N.A.	Temp S.A.
Summer		
Autumn		
Winter		
Spring		

How Come, Huh?
Due to the tilt of the Earth, North America is closer to the sun in summer and farther from it in winter. The slight difference in distance is enough to account for the changes in temperature that we experience.

Science Fair Extensions
11. Describe how the Earth would change if there were no tilt to the axis at all.

Portable Water Cycle

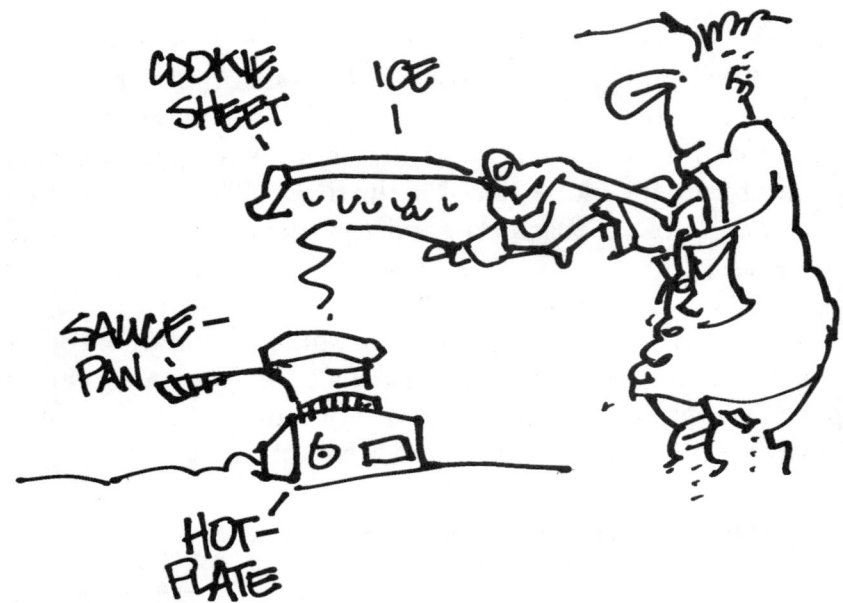

The Experiment

In this lab, you are going to feel radiant heat, see water evaporating, and observe the condensation of warm, moist air, due to changes in temperature. You'll witness the collective accumulation of water into large drops that succumb to the pleadings of gravity as they fall back into the "ocean" of water, also known as a saucepan. In short, you are going to create a mini water cycle in your room.

Materials

1   Quart saucepan
    Ice cubes
    Water
1   Hotplate or stove
1   Metal cookie sheet
1   Plastic tub, 5-quart size or larger
    Adult Supervision

Procedure

1. Completely fill the saucepan with water. With an adult nearby, turn the hotplate or stove on and start to heat the water to boiling.

2. While the water is heating, place 30 to 40 ice cubes on the cookie sheet. The ice cubes will cool the temperature of the sheet significantly.

3. When the water starts to boil, hold the cookie sheet over the evaporating water. Observe what happens to the water vapor as it hits the cookie sheet.

How Come, Huh?

Here's how this lab breaks down into the parts of the water cycle:

Radiant Energy: The hotplate does the work of the sun, providing heat to the water so that it evaporates and rises.

Evaporation: The hot, moist air is expanding and rising the same way that water heated by the sun rises as a vapor into the atmosphere.

Condensation: When the warm air hits the bottom of the cookie sheet, it cools quickly. If you look carefully, sometimes you can see a thin layer of "cloud" near the bottom of the sheet. The water molecules continue to cool and accumulate into large water droplets on the bottom of the pan. When they finally get too heavy to hang onto the bottom of the pan, we have …

Precipitation: Rain. The rain falls back into the pan and the process, as with many things in nature, starts all over again.

Science Fair Extensions

12. Models can always be improved. Create a model that has mountains, a river to collect water, and a big puddle or small ocean to refill.

The Water Cycle

1. Heat from the Sun

Our sun bombards the Earth with radiant energy. Some of this energy causes water in oceans and lakes to evaporate into the atmosphere.

2. Evaporation & Condensation

This water rises into the atmosphere, where it cools to form a thin layer of vapor or clouds of varying sizes and thicknesses.

WATER EVAPORATES

RADIANT ENERGY

PRECIPITATION

4. Water on the Earth's Surface

The rain, snow, etc., flows downward via streams, rivers, and lakes to the oceans of the world. Then, on the next sunny day...

RUNOFF

3. Precipitation

At some point, these clouds are motivated to drop their load in the form of rain, snow, hail, sleet, etc. Collectively, this is called precipitation.

CO$_2$/O$_2$ Exchange

The Experiment

One of the many systems that ecologists study is the carbon dioxide/oxygen exchange that takes place in our environment. Animals breathe in oxygen and exhale carbon dioxide. Plants use carbon dioxide to produce sugar. A by-product of that process is oxygen. Our waste is critical to plants, and we could not survive without their waste. To demonstrate this exchange, you will use a pH indicator called *bromothymol blue*.

For this activity, as you breathe out, the carbon dioxide you exhale will react with water in a baggie to produce carbonic acid. This will slowly acidify the water. The more carbon dioxide you blow into the solution, the more acid is produced, and the lower the pH becomes. The bromothymol blue will turn green when the pH reaches about 6.8. It will turn yellow once the pH drops to 6.0.

Materials

- 1   1-oz. bottle of bromothymol blue
- 1   Straw
- 1   Resealable baggie
- 1   Set of lungs (pre-inserted into body)
      Water
- 1   Bottle of ammonia
- 1   Pipette

Procedure

1. Add a couple of ounces of water to the baggie, and then add two capfuls of bromothymol blue. Seal the baggie and tip it back and forth to mix the two chemicals together.

CO₂/O₂ Exchange

2.   Open the baggie and insert the straw. Holding the baggie tightly around the straw, gently blow into the solution. *DO NOT suck on the straw. You might get sick.*

3.   Observe the color of the solution as you continue to bubble carbon dioxide gas into the solution. The solution should change to a sea-green color first and then, eventually, to a bright yellow.

4.   To return the solution to blue, all you have to do is slowly add drops of a base, such as ammonia, bleach, or almost any other cleaner to the liquid, shaking the baggie after each drop.   Demonstrate this by opening your bottle of ammonia, adding one drop of ammonia liquid to the bromothymol blue solution, and gently shaking the bag. When the pH starts to change, you will see the solution turn from yellow to green and back to blue.

Data & Observations

Record your data in the spaces provided below.

Situation Being Tested	Color of Solution
Starting Color	
First Color Change	
Second Color Change	
Color with Ammonia	

How Come, Huh?

Bromothymol blue is an acid/base indicator that changes color in the pH range of 6.0 to 7.6. When it is in a basic solution with a pH at or above 7.6, it is a blue color. In acidic solutions with a pH of 6.0 or below, it turns yellow. In between, when the solution has nearly neutral pH, the bromothymol blue will appear to be a sea-green color.

Carbon dioxide is a molecule that is slightly acidic. As we exhale this gas into the straw, it bubbles through the solution. As the gas bubbles of carbon dioxide mingle with the other chemicals in the liquid, they cause the pH of the solution to move slightly lower on the pH scale. The first indication is the change in color, from blue to sea-green. As you continue to acidify the solution with your breath, the color changes from green to yellow. These color changes take place because the indicators, themselves, change shape with the addition or subtraction of the hydrogen ions in solution.

Humanoid Factoid

To make this exchange of oxygen with carbon dioxide, your lungs have over 300,000,000 little air sacs, called alveoli (al • vee • oh • lee). Every minute, you breathe in about 13 pints of air.

Science Fair Extensions

13. Design an experiment that will collect air produced by plants and can be indicated by the change in color of bromothymol blue.

The Nitrogen Cycle

1. Nitrogen Gas

78% of our atmosphere is composed of nitrogen gas. It's everywhere. This gas is the foundation for the nitrogen cycle.

NITROGEN GAS

LIGHTNING COSMIC RAD.

4. Decomposing Matter

Dead plants and animals decompose and enrich the soil with nitrogen. As if this were not enough, cyanobacteria also specialize in breaking down this decaying matter and returning nitrogen to the soil.

PLANT & ANIMAL MATTER

SOIL

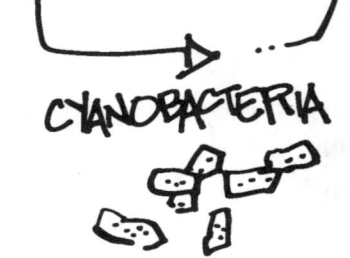

CYANOBACTERIA

2. Energy

Energy, in the form of cosmic radiation from the sun, and lightning zap the nitrogen gas, forming nitrogen-rich compounds that fall to the Earth and are incorporated into the soil.

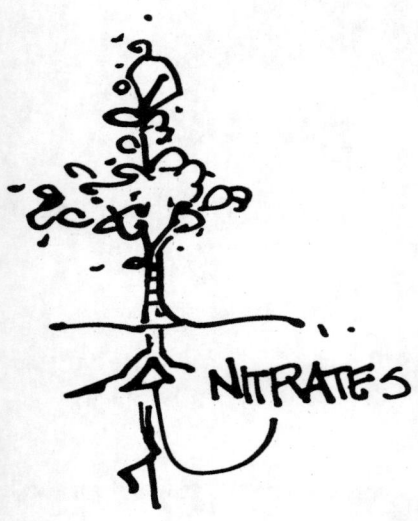

3. Nitrogen Fixation

A curable condition ... just kidding. Certain plants absorb nitrogen from the gas in the soil and produce nitrogen-rich compounds that are present in the plant matter that is eaten by animals.

The Rock Cycle

The Experiment

Another cycle that exists in nature on a very grand scale includes the production, disintegration, and recycling of rocks. This idea is called the rock cycle and is pictured below. We have added all of the major events in the cycle. Your task is to draw arrows showing how each rock group is related to every other rock group. We have inserted one arrow, and now your job is to figure out all of the other possible relationships.

Weathering &
Erosion

Igneous

Weathering &
Erosion

Sediment

Weathering &
Erosion

Sedimentary

Compaction &
Cementation

You can start at any point and wind up back where you started. For example, mud may settle into the bottom of a lake and get smooshed into mudstone. The mudstone gets buried even more and, under the pressure and heat of the Earth, forms slate. Mountain-building in the general area shoves the slate to the core of the Earth, where it is melted, forming magma that erupts onto the surface of the Earth as pumice. The pumice erodes over time and forms fine particles that resemble mud as they are washed downstream into a lake bottom … and so it goes.

Cooling

Melting

Melting

Heat & Pressure

Metamorphic

Heat & Pressure

Heat & Pressure

The Carbon Cycle

The Experiment

If you take all of the cycles and lump them together, you have something called the carbon cycle, which looks something like this.

1. Heat from the Sun

Our sun bombards the Earth with radiant energy. Some of this energy drives the process of photosynthesis, which is the mechanism that plants use to make food.

2. Photosynthesis

The plant uses light energy, water, and carbon dioxide from the air to create complex molecules of starch and other compounds that are stored in the leaves and stems of plants.

4. Respiration

As part of the process of living, animals take in oxygen and give off carbon dioxide. This carbon dioxide is then used by the plants to make more carbon compounds for the herbivores.

CARBON DIOXIDE

CONVERTED TO PROTEIN

3. Metabolism

Along comes a herbivore that nibbles on the plant matter. The carbon that is stored in the leaves and stems is now ingested, rearranged, and stored as protein, carbohydrates, and fat.

Big Idea 3

There are many techniques that we use to observe and study nature.

Field Journal

The Experiment

Many people who work in the field, studying plants, animals, and ecosystems, collect and store information in a field journal. These field journals include notes, drawings, and sometimes plant pressings that are taken in the field.

The purpose of the field journal is to record behaviors, location, colorations, and interactions as they occur. The scientist then takes these notes back to the laboratory for compilation, analysis, and inclusion in the final report. Hence, the field journal is a very valuable tool to have in your repertoire.

Materials

1   Journal page
1   Three-ring notebook
1   Pen or pencil

Procedure

On the next couple of pages, you'll find samples of stock pages that you can copy and use to create your own field journal. Feel free to adapt and modify these pages to suit your personal needs or the specifics of the project that you have chosen to work on.

Field Journal: Animals

Name: _____   Date: _____

Location: _____   Time: _____

Animal Name: _____

Scientific Name: _____

Classification

      Class: _____

      Order: _____

      Family: _____

Coloration/Markings: _____
_____
_____

Behavior: _____
_____
_____
_____
_____
_____
_____

Notes: _____
_____
_____

Field Journal: Plants

Name: _____   Date : _____
Location: _____   Time: _____

Plant Name: _____
Scientific Name: _____

Classification
      Class: _____
      Order: _____
      Family: _____

Height: _____   Occurrence: _____
(metric measurement)   (rare, unusual, common, abundant)

Flower/Fruit
      Monocot/Dicot (Circle one.)
      Color(s): _____
      Arrangement: _____
      Description: _____

Leaf Type
      Arrangement: _____
      Leaf Margin: _____

Notes: _____
_____
_____

Study Plot: Quadrant Survey

The Experiment

When you select a study plot, there are two different ways to study the area that you are interested in. The first, which we will cover in this lab, is to view the plot from above. You divide the area that you are studying into equal sections and record the plant and animal life that you find in each section, using symbols from a key that you have created. The second method, using a transect survey, helps you examine the area from the side and interpret the living things in it from the point of view of how high they are off the ground.

We are going to start with the quadrant survey, which creates a top view of the locations of plant species and allows you to track the tendencies of animals to move through a quadrant.

Materials

12 Stakes
1 Hammer
1 Roll of twine
1 Meterstick
1 Notebook with pencil

Procedure

1. Select your study plot. It should be 3 meters by 3 meters square.

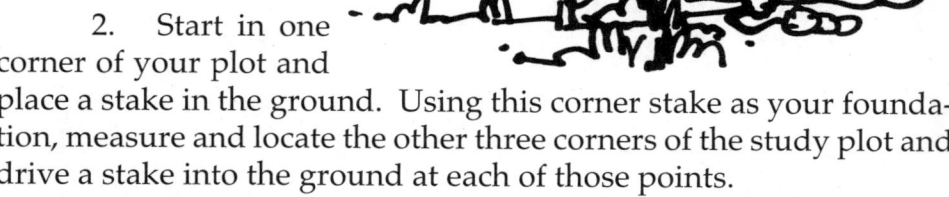

2. Start in one corner of your plot and place a stake in the ground. Using this corner stake as your foundation, measure and locate the other three corners of the study plot and drive a stake into the ground at each of those points.

3. Once you have the corner stakes in place (show them with solid dots to begin a diagram below), measure and stake one-meter marks along each side of the study plot (to be shown with hollow dots in the diagram.)

4. Now that all twelve stakes are placed in the ground, tie the end of the twine to the <u>top</u> of the stake that is in the bottom-left corner. Keep the rest of the twine on the roll. Walk straight up the row of stakes and wrap the twine with a single wrap around each stake to hold the twine in place.

5. When you get to the top of the row, move over to the next section and go back down the way that you came. Wrap the twine around the stakes as you go.

6. Using the pattern on the next page, follow the arrow direction and make a complete grid of nine one-meter squares that are outlined with twine.

Study Plot:
Quadrant Survey

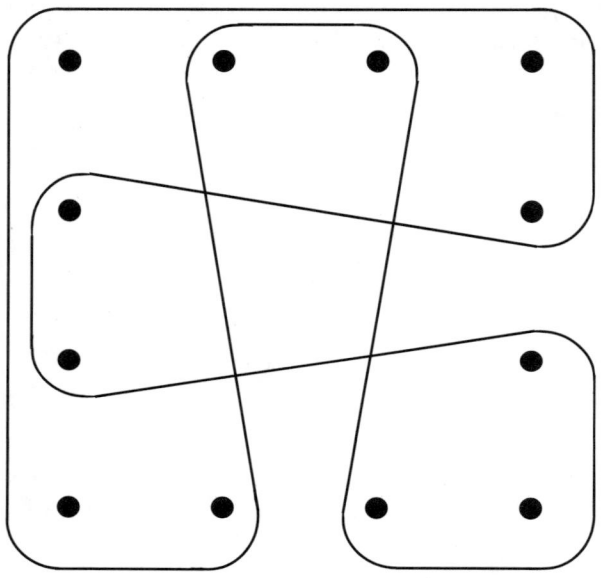

7.   Now you are ready to construct a plant key. Identify as many of the different kinds of plants that are located in the study plot as you can. Assign each plant a symbol. To make things easier, we suggest that you use four basic designs—a square, a triangle, a circle, and a dash. Each of these designs can then be further adapted to show solid, shaded, and hollow versions. This will give you the ability to identify, plot, and record 12 different plant species, which should be more than enough, in your study plot.

8.   Once you have the plants in order, you can observe insects, amphibians, reptiles, birds, and small mammals that may wander into your study plot. Because these are animals and they are constantly on the move, you do not need to plot a fixed position. Simply keep track of what you see.

Data & Observations

When you are done, your study plot should look something like the illustration shown here.

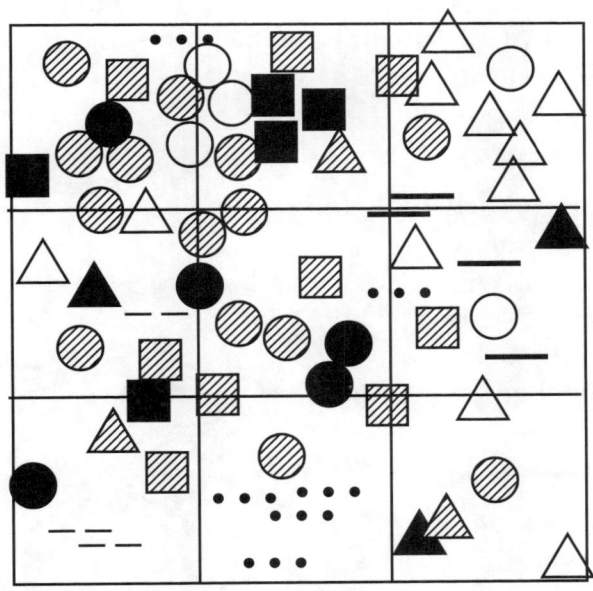

Science Fair Extensions

14.   Figure out a way to rig an aerial view of your study plot, take a photograph of it, and compare the accuracy of how you plotted the plants with the photo of the study plot.

Study Plot: Transect Survey

The Experiment

When you transect something, you cut across it and look at a slice of the area. A transect survey is the same idea. As you conducted the quadrant survey, you got a very good idea of how the plants arranged themselves on the ground and how much space they took up as they grew. What you could not tell about your study plot was how the plants arranged themselves vertically—which plants were taller than others and which plants took up residence in the shade of other plants.

To remedy this situation, you are going to construct a transect survey and draw a picture of how the plants in a single section stack up in a vertical sense.

Materials

2   Stakes, each 4-feet long
1   Hammer
1   Roll of twine
1   Pair of scissors
1   Meterstick
1   Notebook with pencil

Procedure

1.   Select your study plot. It should be 3 meters long.

2.   Start on one side of your section and drive a wooden stake into the ground.

3. Using this corner stake as your foundation, measure and locate the other side of the study plot and drive a stake into the ground at that point.

4. Drive each stake into the ground so that exactly one meter of each one is sticking up out of the ground.

5. Measuring from the ground up, mark the stakes at 30, 60, and 90 centimeters. Tie one end of the twine to one stake at the 30-cm mark, run it across the study plot to the 30-cm mark on the other stake, and tie it off. Do this two more times at 60 and 90 centimeters, respectively.

6. You should now have two stakes in the ground with three parallel sections of twine marking the 30-, 60-, and 90-centimeter levels.

Study Plot: Transect Survey

Data & Observations

Using the box on the previous page, draw the plants that you find in your transect survey. Pay special attention to how tall they are, how much room they take up from side to side, which plants are found near the top, and which are found near the bottom of the survey.

How Come, Huh?

The transect survey gives you a way to examine the vertical dynamics of a section of an ecosystem. Plants are always trying to optimize their chances for survival and, contrary to popular thought, it is not always the tallest, widest, or most prolific plant that survives. A lot of times, plants thrive in shady areas. Shade protects them from exposure to the sun, reduces the amount of evaporation, and provides moist soil for a longer period of time.

By examining a transect survey and noting where different kinds of plants appear, you can infer what is best for their survival.

Science Fair Extensions

15. Make a series of ten transect surveys, each being 3 meters long and moving in a straight line. Compare how the plant diversity changes or remains the same. Note any changes as you travel from one area to another.

16. Super-size this lab and take it into the deciduous or coniferous forest. At this level, the forest has what are called canopies, or layers of plants. There are usually three or four canopies, and different kinds of plants thrive in the different layers of the forest.

Study Plot: Trackway Grid

The Experiment

A trackway grid is a safe way to set a "trap" for small mammals, birds, and reptiles, and possibly some amphibians. This kind of a "trap" catches tracks, and that's it. There is no harm to the animals. In fact, they may not even know that they are part of a science experiment.

Materials

4 Stakes
1 Hammer
1 Rake
1 Roll of twine
1 Meterstick
1 Notebook with pencil
   Bait

Procedure

1. Select your study plot. It should be 3 meters by 3 meters square, located in an area that is completely devoid of plant matter. Shores of a lake, an open area in a meadow, a sandy beach alongside a stream—all are great places to select.

2. Start in one corner of your plot and place a stake in the ground. Using this corner stake as your foundation, measure and locate the other three corners of the study plot. Drive stakes into the ground at those points.

Study Plot: Trackway Grid

3. Once you have the corner stakes in place, take the rake and soften up the ground. Remove sticks, rocks, and any litter. Leave plants that are in your area. Wrap the twine around the first stake and make a complete loop around the four stakes so that you have a giant square.

4. Place the bait in the middle of the trackway grid. The bait can be bread, popcorn, pieces of meat, or whatever you think will attract animals to the grid. Rake over your footprints so that there are no marks inside the grid.

5. Leave the grid overnight and come back to it in the morning. Inspect the grid and identify and record the position of the different tracks that have been left behind.

How Come, Huh?

The tracks will give you several pieces of information about the area that you have chosen to study. You will be able to discern what kinds of animals visit your grid, how big they are, and if you are a frequent visitor to your grid, what time of day they prefer.

Science Fair Extensions

17. Break your study into two halves, daytime and nocturnal (night) time. Compare the animals that visit your trackway grid during each half of the day. Make a list of animals that are active during the day and those that prefer to come out and play at night.

18. If you get good impressions of some larger mammals, figure out how to make plaster tracks. Collect several specimens for your study report.

Butterfly Ranch

The Experiment

Insects go through a series of physical changes. This series of changes is called a metamorphosis. Typically, a description of this process starts with an egg, which is laid by an adult insect, and proceeds through a series of changes to produce another adult. In this case, we are going to start in the middle of the process with a pupa, which is a butterfly larva that has spun a cocoon to metamorphose inside.

Materials

1   Butterfly pupa
1   Aquarium

Procedure

1. Butterflies can be ordered from a variety of sources. Check the Web, your local pet store, and any of a number of catalog companies. The pupa will arrive with a set of instructions, ready to be placed in an aquarium.

2. Read the instructions for your particular butterfly larva and follow them. Time to hatch is usually between 3 to 6 weeks, depending on the variety of butterfly.

3. When the butterfly emerges and dries, place it in the open so that it can zip on out into the world and enjoy life.

How Come, Huh?

The life cycles of most insects have four distinct stages. The egg, laid by an adult, waits until the conditions are favorable for survival. (There's no sense hatching in the middle of a snowstorm.) When the warm weather and moisture of spring arrive, the egg hatches and produces a larva, or caterpillar. The caterpillar eats and eats and eats, and stores up energy in the form of fat. When the conditions are again advantageous, the caterpillar weaves a cocoon. Inside the cocoon, the larva becomes a beautiful butterfly. When the butterfly has fully metamorphosed, it breaks out of the cocoon, dries its wings, and takes off in the sunshine.

Science Fair Extensions

19. There are many other kinds of insects available to study. Check online and see what you can come up with.

20. Plant a butterfly garden to attract butterflies to your home.

Mealworm Farming

The Experiment

Mealworms are readily available at any bait shop, they reproduce quickly and easily, and they will allow you to observe the changes that take place in insects from a slightly different point of view. Instead of four distinct stages, as in the butterfly life cycle, you will observe only three changes. Then, the adult insect increases in size by going through what are called instars.

Instars are simply larger incarnations of the same insect. Imagine that your puppy would become very still one day, and then all of a sudden would shed all of its skin and become bigger. That is what some insects do. They shed their skin and emerge from the instar with a larger container.

Materials

35 Mealworms
1   Cup of bran
1   4-6 oz. jar with lid
    Water

Procedure

1. Place the cup of bran inside the jar. Measure your mealworms' lengths and determine an average size. Record your data on a separate sheet. Drop your mealworms into the bran.

2. Add enough water to moisten the bran, but do not get it soaking wet. In fact, it is better if you add water to only one side of the bran and leave the rest of it dry.

3. Once a week for four weeks, empty the jar, collect your mealworms, look for instar casings, and measure your mealworms. Compare the size of your mealworms each week.

4. When you are all done with the experiment, you can release the beetles and leftover mealworms into your backyard, where they will make an easy and tasty meal for the birds in your neighborhood. Either that, or you can go fishing with your newly culti-vated bait.

How Come, Huh?

Not all insects go through a traditional metamorphosis. Crickets, mealworms, and other insects simply go from egg to larva, to larger larva, to larger larva, to adult. These increasingly larger versions of the same thing are called instars. In the case of the mealworm, the eggs turn into larvae, which go through instars. When each insect is ready to reproduce, it becomes a beetle, mates, and lays more eggs for the next go-around.

Science Fair Extensions

21. Head out into a grassy field and collect as many different kinds of crickets as you can find. This is another insect that goes through instars. The instar in this case turns out to be the actual adult cricket. (Weird group of animals, these arthropods!)

Pond Scope

The Experiment

If you would like to venture off land and into water (streams, ponds, or shallow tidepools), a coffee can that has been modified will act as a hand-viewer to allow you to see underwater critters, plants, and organisms more clearly.

Materials

1   Coffee can
1   Can opener
1   Large rubberband
1   Sheet of plastic wrap

Procedure

1. Cut out both ends of the coffee can and clean it with soap and water.

2. Tear off a sheet of plastic wrap that is larger than the openings of the can. Place the plastic wrap over one end of the can and fix it in place with the rubberband.

3. Head out to the pond, stream, or tidepool that you would like to investigate, and plop the covered end of the can into the water, holding the can about halfway down in the water. Do not let it fill with water.

4. Use the can to look at things in the water.

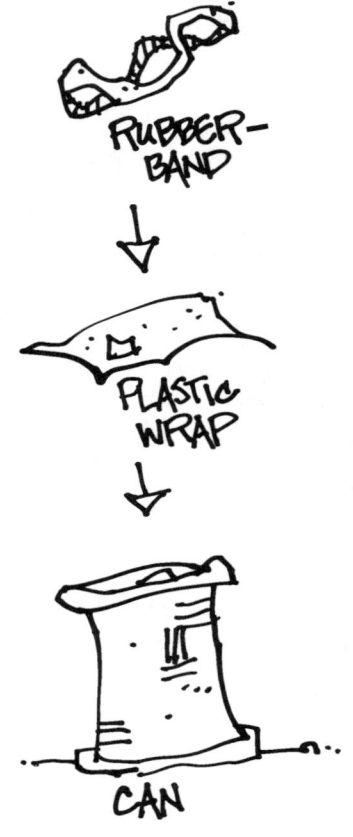

RUBBER-BAND

PLASTIC WRAP

CAN

The Original World Wide Web • B. K. Hixson

How Come, Huh?

The pond scope acts just like a diving mask. When the scope is placed in the water, the light images coming up from the bottom of the pond are refracted through the plastic and into the air. Because our eyes are designed to interpret light that is traveling through air better than light that is traveling through water, we see the object with greater clarity.

Because the pond scope is portable, you can look for plants and animals and, when you find one, you can pass the scope to your friends. If you were to put a diving mask on, it would do the same exact thing.

Science Fair Extensions

22.   Go for a ride on a glass-bottomed boat. This is the same idea, just on a bigger scale.

23.   You can make a family-sized pond scope if you have a popcorn tin left over from the holidays. Simply cut out the bottom of the 5-gallon can, cover it, and you are off to the races.

Suet Balls and Peanut Butter Pinecones

The Experiment

Suet is animal fat. It is the stuff that is left over when you trim your steaks. Peanut butter pinecones are not native to any particular region in the U.S.; however, if you have a can of peanut butter and a big pinecone, you can make one to hang in your yard.

This lab is designed to show you how to make two outdoor tree ornaments that will attract birds to your home and make it easier for you to birdwatch.

Materials

1   Pile of animal fat
1   Bag of birdseed
1   Pinecone
1   Jar of peanut butter
1   Knife
1   Bowl
1   Roll of twine or heavy string

Procedure

1. Snip off 3 feet of twine and tie it to the top end of the pinecone. Cones from Ponderosa, Sugar, and White Pine trees are the best varieties for this activity. They are large and easy to fill. However, if you live in a region where these do not grow, almost anything will attract birds.

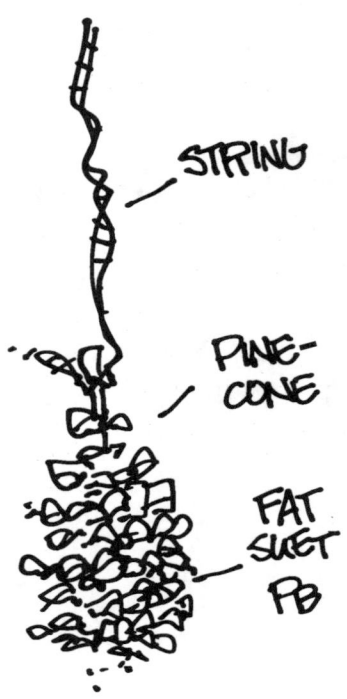

STRING

PINE-CONE

FAT
SUET
PB

2. Using the knife, scoop the suet and the fresh peanut butter into the bowl. Add an ample supply of commercial birdseed, and stir it into the mixture with the knife.

3. Once the fat, peanut butter, and birdseed have been mixed together, use the knife to apply it to the nooks and crannies of the pinecone. When it is full of the mixture, tie it to the limb of a large tree outside and enjoy the parade of birds that will come to visit your buffet offerings.

How Come, Huh?

Birds like seeds and fat. If someone were standing on the street corner, handing out hamburgers fresh off a hot grill, we are confident that there would be a couple of takers. It's the same thing here.

Science Fair Extensions

24. There are commercial seedballs available at most home improvement centers, pet stores, and pet sections of major department stores. Compare the bird-attracting capacity of your homemade seedball to that of the commercial varieties.

Big Idea 4

There are many techniques and tools that can be used to collect specimens and study nature.

Plant Press

The Experiment

A plant press is a tool used by botanists and ecologists in the field to collect and preserve plant specimens. It can be used for herbaceous plants, as well as those with woody stems.

The purpose of a plant press is to press, dry, and preserve plant specimens so that they can be studied at a later date. To do this, the plant is collected in the field, cleaned, placed between sheets of newspaper, and then squished between sheets of cardboard or plywood and held in place with nylon straps. This lab will give you directions on how to make your own plant press and also how to create a high-quality herbarium specimen for your collection.

Materials

2   Adjustable nylon straps
1   Large newspaper
1   Pair of scissors
1   X-Acto knife
21 Sheets of corrugated cardboard,
      11 inches by 14 inches or larger
2   Sheets of plywood,
      11 inches by 14 inches by 1/2-inch thick
20 Sheets of newsprint,
      11 inches by 14 inches or larger
1   Can of spray fixative
1   Pencil or pen
    Blotter paper
    Index cards

Procedure

1. Place one sheet of plywood on the cardboard and, using the X-Acto knife, cut the cardboard so that it is the exact same size as the sheet of plywood. Do this until you have 21 sheets of cardboard prepared.

Plant Press

2. Once you have the cardboard cut, you are going to want to do the same thing with a section of newsprint from the local paper.

Select a section that has complete sheets. Place the cardboard on the paper and cut out 20 sheets that open up.

3. To assemble your plant press, place a single sheet of plywood on the table. Add a sheet of cardboard, a sheet of newsprint, another sheet of cardboard, another sheet of newsprint, and continue this until all of the pieces of cardboard and newsprint have been stacked on top of one another. The finished product should look like a giant paper sandwich.

4. When you place the final piece of cardboard on the pile, top it off with the second piece of plywood.

5. Using adjustable nylon straps that are common to camping sections in recreational stores, wrap the straps around the pile of wood, cardboard, and paper. Slide the end of the strap into the buckle and tighten it so that the press is compact and so that nothing will fall out.

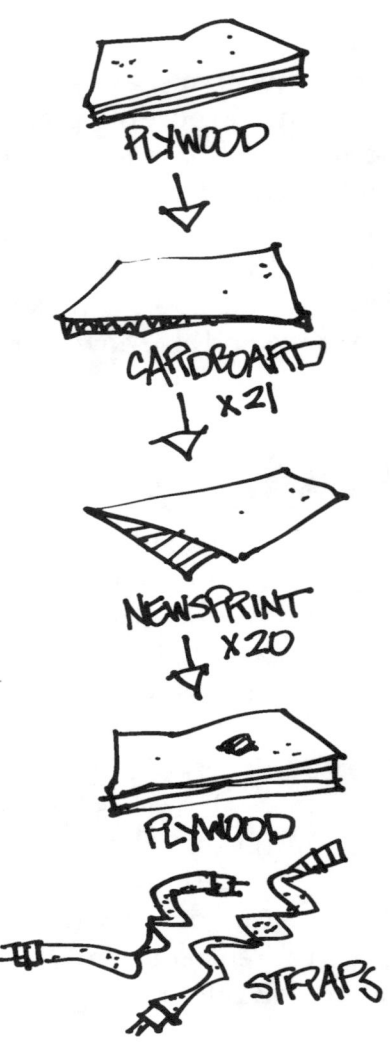

6. Take the press with you into the field. When you find a specimen that you would like to collect, open the press up. If your specimen is a herbaceous plant, gently remove the entire specimen (roots, stem, and flower) from the ground. Wash the soil from the roots and dry them. If your specimen is a tree or shrub, cut a section that will fit into the press.

7. Select the section of the press that you would like to use to press the plant. Open up the newspaper and place the plant inside. Close the newspaper, place a piece cardboard on the plant, and gently squish it into place. Then, reassemble the press and tighten the straps as far as they will go.

8. Continue to collect plants and place them inside your plant press. When you are done, tighten the press one more time and set it an area where it will remain warm and dry.

9. Check the plant press every couple of days. As the plants dry, they will require less space, so you'll need to tighten the straps to keep the pressure on the plants. They should be dry and ready to mount in two or three weeks.

Plant Press

10. When the plants are dry, gently remove them from the newsprint and spray one side of each with a spray fixative. Place the plants on the blotter paper and place the blotter paper inside the newsprint.

11. Repeat this process for all of the plants that you have collected. When they have all been glued and fixed to the paper, reassemble your plant press and let the specimens dry to the page for one more day.

12. Remove the specimens from the plant press and label them with the information in the section below, which can be written on prepared specimen cards.

Data & Observations

Here and on separate cards, record the following for each plant that you press.

Common Name: _____ Date Collected: _____
Scientific Name: _____ Location Collected: _____
Your Name: _____ Specimen #: _____

How Come, Huh?

The press dries the plants, and barring rough handling, fires, floods, or wandering herbivores, the collection should be good for many, many years.

Leaf Rubbings

The Experiment

If you do not want to collect, press, dry, and mount specimens, the other option is to simply take a rubbing of a leaf or a flower. This alternative happens to be the focus of this lab.

Materials

1   Stack of drawing paper
1   Pencil or crayon
1   Clipboard
1   3-ring notebook
    Specimens

Procedure

1. Place the specimen on the clipboard and cover it with a sheet of paper.

2. Using the side of a pencil or the edge of a crayon, rub the surface of the paper that is on top of the specimen. This will create an impression of the specimen.

3. Use one sheet per specimen, and keep all of your rubbings in a notebook.

Data & Observations

When you are done with each rubbing, label it with the same information that you would use to label a pressed plant specimen.

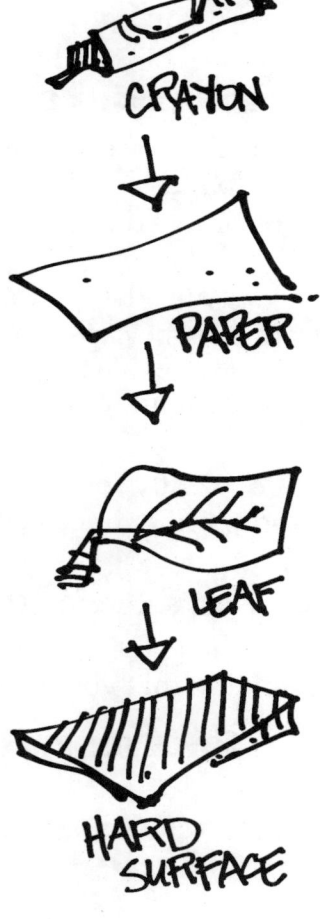

Spore Prints

The Experiment

Mushrooms reproduce by producing spores from the undersides of their caps. These spores will fall directly onto a piece of paper and can be preserved with a spray fixative as a spore print.

Materials

1   Mushroom cap
1   Can of spray fixative
1   Sheet of blotter paper
1   Pencil

Procedure

1. Place the mushroom cap on the piece of paper and leave it undisturbed for four or five days.

2. After the allotted time, remove the mushroom cap and you will see a circular design that looks like spokes from a wheel, radiating out from the center.

3. Gently spray the spore print with the fixative. Use one sheet per spore print and keep your specimens in a notebook.

Data & Observations

When you are done with the spore print, label it with the same information that you would use to label a pressed plant specimen or a rubbing.

Bug Board

The Experiment

This is probably the easiest way for you to collect insects. Find a board that is 8 to 12 inches wide and about 3 feet long. Place it in a grassy area for 2 or 3 days. When you come back and lift up the board, you will find all kinds of critters that have taken up residence in the new condo you created.

Materials

1   Board, 8 inches wide by 3 feet long
1   Grassy area
1   Collecting jar

Procedure

1. Find a grassy area that is relatively undisturbed. Place the board down on the grass.

2. Return in a few days and flip the board over. What you will discover is that all kinds of invertebrates, insects, millipedes, caterpillars, and other creatures like a dark, damp area to hang out in.

3. Using your fingers or a pooter, which we will cover in a couple of labs, gather the bugs that are underneath the board, and add them to your collection.

Science Fair Extensions

25. Go on a field trip in your neighborhood and find large stones, rocks, boards, pieces of cardboard, old tires, and anything else that has been sitting for awhile, and flip them over. You are bound to find a treasure of goodies.

Insect Net

The Experiment

If you are not fond of flipping old boards, rocks, or tires over and chasing your bugs that way, then you can always revert to the old-fashioned insect net.

Materials

1   Wire hanger
1   Wooden dowel, 4 feet long
1   Roll of cheesecloth
1   Pair of scissors
1   Roll of masking tape
1   Sewing machine
1   Collecting jar
    Index cards

Procedure

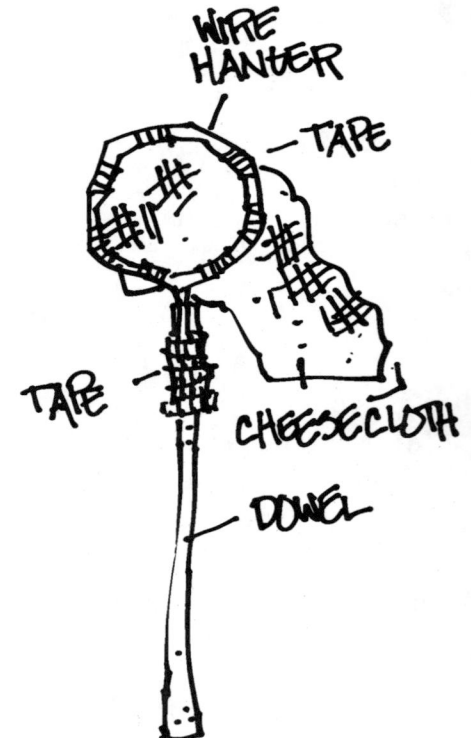

1. Bend the wire hanger into a loop shape, with the top part of the hanger straightened out. It should look something like what is shown in the picture at the right.

2. Cut a three-foot section of cheesecloth. Cheesecloth has multiple layers, so separate it until you have just two layers together.

3. Sew two of the three sides of the cheesecloth closed with a sewing machine. Leave one side open.

4. Attach the open end of the cheesecloth to the wire hanger and tape it in place in the manner shown in the illustration above.

5. Attach the two wire leads to the wooden dowel to complete your insect net. Tape the leads down. If you have a hard time keeping your net on your dowel, you can always drill a hole in the center of the dowel and insert the wire leads into it.

6. The best way to use an insect net is to walk through grassy areas, moving the net back and forth with a wide, sweeping motion. About every 10 sweeps or so, look inside the net and see if you have anything of interest.

7. Slide the collecting jar inside the net and collect the bugs you want to keep. Label them with the information shown in the *Data & Observations* section. All of the information can be written onto prepared specimen cards.

Data & Observations

Write the following information on specimen cards:

Common Name: _____ Date Collected: _____
Scientific Name: _____ Location Collected: _____
Your Name: _____ Specimen #: _____

Pooter

The Experiment

We are not sure who invented the name of this thing, but we assure you that if you talk with any entomologists and you ask them about a pooter, they will know exactly what you are talking about.

A pooter is a tool used by entomologists (folks who study bugs) and naturalists to collect small, hard-to-nab bugs. A lot of bugs are too little or too fragile to pick up with a pair of tweezers or your fingers, so you use a pooter, which is a kind of bug vacuum. Here's how you make one:

Materials

1   Quart jar with lid
1   Screwdriver, Phillips
1   Hammer
1   Rubber hose, 8 inches long,
        1/4-inch in diameter
1   Rubber hose, 12 inches long,
        1/4-inch in diameter
1   Rubberband
1   Piece of gauze,
        1 inch by 1 inch

Procedure

1. Remove the lid from the quart jar and, using the Phillips screwdriver, punch two holes, one opposite the other.

2. Select one hole, thread the 12-inch piece of rubber hose into the top of the lid, and pull it down about one inch.

3. Thread the other hose through the other hole, and pull it about one inch through the lid.

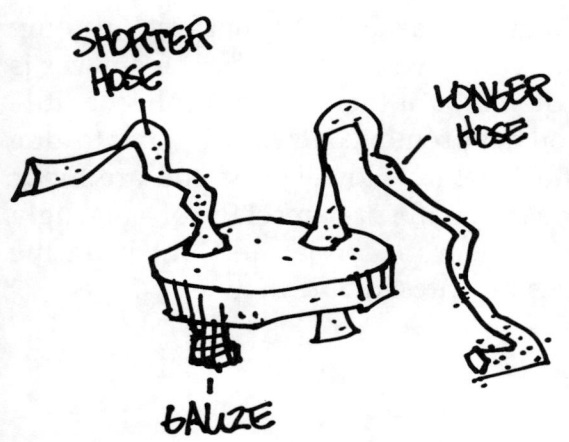

SHORTER HOSE

LONGER HOSE

GAUZE

4. Take the gauze and fold it over the end of the shorter hose that is inside the lid. Hold the fabric over the hole with a rubberband. This fabric is designed to be a kind of filter that prevents bugs in the jar from being sucked up into your mouth.

5. Screw the lid onto the jar, and you are ready to go.

6. A pooter, as we mentioned in the introduction, is a bug vacuum. Locate a small, hard-to-grab bug. Hold the end of the long hose near the bug, and put the end of the shorter hose into your mouth. When you are ready to collect the bug, hold the hose end right near the bug and suck in quickly. The air moving into the jar will nab the bug and pull it in. With luck, the fabric over the end of the hose that you are sucking on will keep the bug from going up into your mouth.

7. Collect the bugs you want to keep, and label them.

Spreading Board

The Experiment

OK, the question that begs to be asked is, "What are you going to do with all of the bugs that you have collected?" The answer is obvious: Preserve them and then mount them. If you collect a little bug, all you have to do after you have removed it from the jar is to glue it to a piece of cardboard and label it. However, if you are lucky enough to capture a butterfly, a dragonfly or damsel fly, or a big, ugly moth, you will want to remove it from the jar and put it on the spreading board so that it dries in a presentable manner.

Materials

1   Piece of plywood,
    11 inches by 8 inches by 1/2-inch thick
2   Balsawood strips,
    1 inch by 8 inches by 1/4-inch thick
1   Box of pins
1   Bottle of wood glue
4   Finishing nails
1   Hammer
1   Pair of scissors
1   Sheet of chipboard

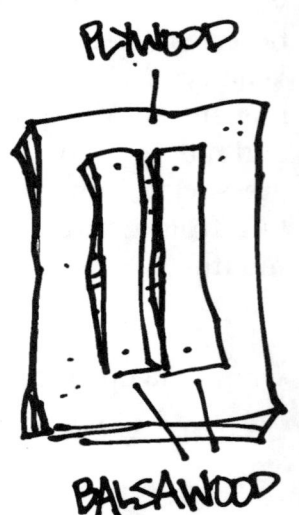

Procedure

1. Glue the two strips of balsawood on the plywood so that they are parallel and about 1/4-inch away from each other. Use the illustration at the right as a guide. Secure the glued pieces with a finishing nail at each end.

2. When you catch a bug that is large, particularly one with wings, you will want to pin it out on the spreading board so that it dries in a presentable position.

3. Remove the dead bug from the killing jar. Place the body in the center of the two balsawood strips so that it hangs down between them. Position the wings so that they are flat on the balsawood.

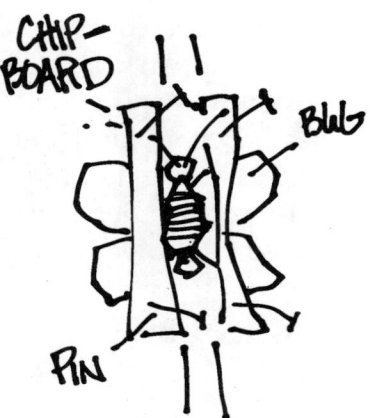

4. Cut two strips of chipboard that are each 3 inches long and about 1/2-inch wide. Place the chipboard over the wing to hold it down, and pin both sides of the chipboard to hold it in place.

5. Let the bug dry for about a week, and then you can add it to your collection. Label each bug with the following information, which can be written on a prepared specimen card or on scrap paper.

Data & Observations

Record the following on a prepared specimen card:

Common Name:_____ Date Collected:_____
Scientific Name:_____ Location Collected:_____
Your Name:_____ Specimen #:_____

Pondwater Filter

The Experiment

We've been busy collecting bugs in nets, tracks in the mud, and plants that happen to be close to the trail, but what about critters in the water? Pondwater is full of a whole host of microorganisms that swim in lakes, streams, and hang out in great abundance, just daring someone to notice them.

To collect these little critters, you can construct a modified plankton net that we call a pondwater filter.

Materials

1   Plastic pint jar
1   Pair of old nylons
1   Rubberband
1   Drill with bit
1   Nylon rope, 8 feet long
1   Microscope
1   Coat hanger

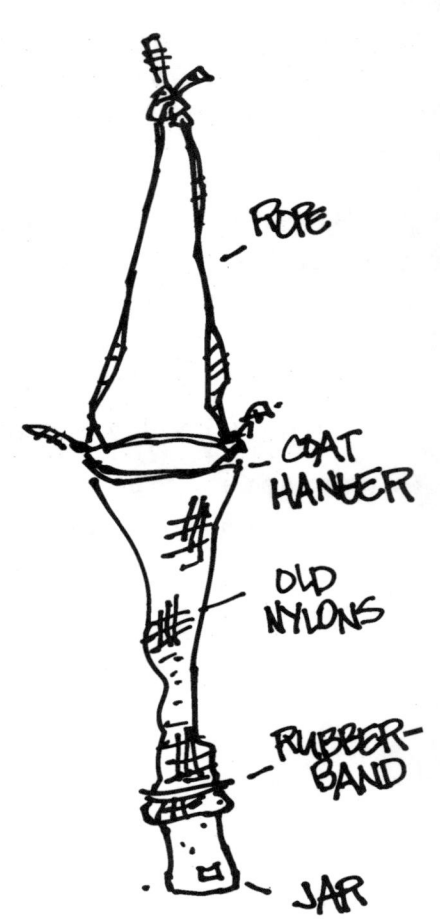

Procedure

1. Using the drill, make two holes near the top edge of the plastic jar. The holes should be just big enough for the rope to fit through.

2. Make an overhand knot in the end of the rope, and pull it through the hole until it is snug. Feed the other end of the rope through the other hole, make a second overhand knot, and pull it back through the hole. Use the illustration at the right as a guide.

3. Cut a section from the nylons. The section should be big enough to fit snugly over the top of the jar. Use the rubberband to hold the nylons in place, kind of like the covering on a drum.

4. Take your pondwater filter out into a pond and start dragging it behind you, allowing lots of water to flow into and out of the jar. After 5 minutes, take a sample of the water you have collected and look at it under the microscope.

How Come, Huh?

The nylons allow really little organisms to flow into the jar and be caught. Larger ones cannot fit inside.

Science Fair Extensions

26. Acquire a commercial plankton net and take a sample from the same area at about the same time of year. Compare its effectiveness at catching critters to that of your homemade pondwater filter.

Plaster Tracks

The Experiment

Mammals, particularly large ones, such as deer, elks, bears, and coyotes, as well as some smaller animals, such as rabbits, marmots, the occasional chubby squirrel, and skunks leave nice-sized tracks when they are walking along river banks, lake shores, through muddy sections of meadows, or through the trackway grid that you baited. Examining these prints can tell you how large the animal is, if it is hurt, what direction it was traveling in, and how fast it was traveling. You can also collect these prints using plaster, which is the direction in which we are headed in this lab.

Materials

1   Box of plaster of Paris
1   Container of water
5   Tongue depressors
1   Mixing container (cup)
    Several chipboard strips,
        3 inches by 11 inches
1   Box of paperclips
    Baggies, reclosable

Procedure

1. When you find a track that you would like to cast, form a ring, using the chipboard. Roll it into a loop, and clip the top and bottom with the paperclip, as is shown in the illustration at the right.

2. Gently push the chipboard frame into the soil around the track, forming a border to hold the plaster of Paris.

3. Add half a cup of plaster to your mixing cup, and slowly add water to the plaster. Stir the water into the plaster. Continue adding water until the plaster is the consistency of pudding. Make sure there are no lumps or dry pockets in your mixture.

4. Gently pour the wet plaster into the track. Fill the track and the chipboard border to the top. The wetter the plaster, the better the impression, but also the longer it takes to dry. Let the plaster dry for at least half an hour.

5. When the top of the cast is hard to the touch, gently lift the entire mold from the ground. Gently brush the dirt, sticks, needles, and other debris away from the surface of the track. Peel the chipboard border away from the track.

Plaster Tracks

6.   Label your plaster cast with the following information, which can be written on a prepared specimen card.

Data & Observations

Record the following information to label each cast:

Common Name: _____ Date Collected: _____
Scientific Name: _____ Location Collected: _____
Your Name: _____ Specimen #: _____

Science Fair Extensions

27.   If you are lucky enough to get a good, deep trackway from a small animal, you can record the entire trackway. Use the border of a box lid and squish it into a representative portion of the trackway. Mix up a huge batch of plaster, and gently pour the plaster over the whole area that you wish to record. When the plaster is dry, lift the entire section up and out of the ground. You will not only have a track, but you will also have trackways, showing speed, direction, and the size of the animal that left the tracks.

Big Idea 5

Plants and animals have evolved and adapted to be able to survive in a variety of environments and biomes.

Chubby Cactus

The Experiment

Cacti not only live, but thrive in very harsh environments. A desert has less than 10 inches of rain per year, and when that rain comes down, it comes in large quantities very quickly. What this means to the cacti is that they not only have to figure out ways to collect water quickly, but they must also store it efficiently and use it sparingly.

The next four labs in this book will give you an idea of how the family of plants called cacti can accomplish this feat.

Materials

1   Roll of paper towels
1   Cookie sheet
6   Twist ties
    Sun
    Water

Procedure

1. Take a single paper towel and roll it tightly into a column. Use twist ties at both ends and in the middle to keep it from unrolling.

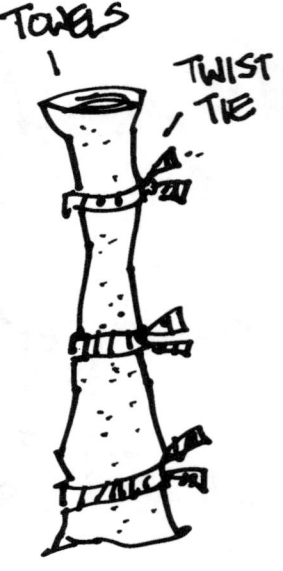

2. Peel off 10 more paper towels and stack them into a big pile. Roll them into a tight bundle and secure them with 3 more twist ties at the ends and in the middle. Use the illustration at the right as a guide.

3. Soak both bundles in water, and set them on a cookie sheet. Along with the two bundles, include a wet paper towel that has been spread out flat.

Data & Observations

Put the cookie sheet in the sun and compare and record the feel of the three different paper towels at the times identified below:

Time (minutes)	Amount of Moisture Retained		
0			
5			
10			
15			
20			

How Come, Huh?

What you should have noticed is that the single, flat towel dried out the quickest. The single, rolled towel was next, and the thick roll of ten towels dried out the most slowly. Cacti are designed like the last set of towels. They have a thick stem with few branches and no leaves. This design reduces the amount of surface area exposed to the sun, and it reduces water loss, too.

Science Fair Extensions

28. Calculate the surface area of a cactus, and then determine its weight. Compare the measurements to those of a deciduous tree with lots of leaves.

Waxy Cactus

The Experiment

Thick stems are the first trick to storing water. Once you get it stored, you want to keep it from transpiring up into the atmosphere. One of the best ways to do this is to cover the stem with a waxy coating—an idea that was stolen by another native of the deserts, the creosote bush.

You can smell a creosote bush from 200 yards away, and this is the best way to identify it. However, when you walk up to it and feel its leaves, you'll also notice that they are very, very waxy.

Materials

1   Roll of paper towels
1   Roll of wax paper
1   Cookie sheet
6   Twist ties
    Sun
    Water

Procedure

1. Peel off 6 paper towels and stack them into a big pile. Roll them into a tight bundle and secure the bundle with 3 more twist ties at the ends and in the middle.

2. Do the same thing with a second stack of 6 paper towels so that you have two sets ready to go.

3. Soak both bundles in water and set them on a cookie sheet. Take one of the bundles and wrap a single sheet of wax paper around it. Then, secure it with a twist tie.

Data & Observations

Put the cookie sheet in the sun, and compare the feel of the two different bundles of paper towels at the times identified below:

Time (minutes)	Amount of Moisture Retained	
0		
5		
10		
15		
20		

How Come, Huh?

Water is a polar molecule, and wax is not. What this means to the casual observer is that wax and water do not mix very well. If you add a wax coating to an apple, it will stay plump longer because the water is prevented from evaporating through the skin. This is why so much of the produce that you buy in the grocery store, especially cucumbers, apples, and peppers, has that feel.

Cacti figured this out a long time before the grocers did. A coating of wax on the stem in the case of a cactus, and leaves in the case of a creosote bush, prevents a lot of water loss.

Expando Cactus

The Experiment

With infrequent rains and the constant need for water, the cactus has to adapt to take advantage of the water when it arrives. To do this, it has a special ability to increase the diameter of its stem to accommodate the influx of water when a cloud burst sets upon the desert landscape.

This lab is designed to help you understand how this is possible with such a thick, stumpity stem.

Materials

1   Sheet of construction paper
1   Stapler
1   Oblong balloon
1   Measuring tape

Procedure

1. Fold the construction paper accordion style, lengthwise, using one-inch folds.

PAPER CYLINDER

2. When you get the whole paper folded, staple the edges together so that you have a cylinder that is crinkly. Use the illustration at the right as a guide.

3. When you hold the paper cylinder in your hand, you will notice that the cylinder has the ability to shrink and expand with its folds. This is the design that the cactus incorporated to accommodate water flow.

4. Insert an oblong balloon into the paper cylinder. Take a deep breath and inflate the balloon. Notice what happens to the sides of the paper cylinder when you do this. Measure the diameter of the balloon when it is inflated.

5. Release the air from the balloon and observe what happens to the sides of the paper cylinder. This is what happens to a cactus when there is little to no water for long periods of time. Measure the diameter of the balloon when it is empty, and compare that diameter to that of the inflated balloon.

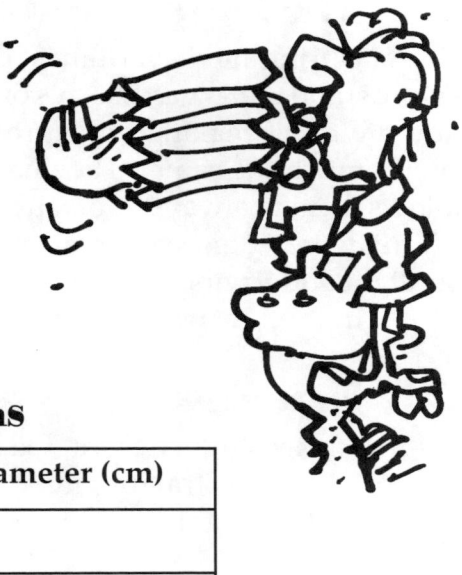

Data & Observations

Balloon (Cactus)	Diameter (cm)
Full of Air	
Empty	

How Come, Huh?

The stem of the cactus expands and contracts, depending on how much water is available in the environment. The paper cylinder did the same thing, as the air was added and released.

In a desert environment, there is less than 10 inches of rain annually. However, the rain is not consistent. To adapt to this kind of environment, the cactus has an extensive root system that sometimes reaches over 100 feet from the base of the cactus. When the rains do come, these roots swell and absorb as much water as they can. The water is then transported to the stem, where it is stored until the next rainstorm hits.

Medieval Cactus

The Experiment

During medieval times, there were lots of forts, spears, and swords, and there was also lots of aggressive behavior toward anyone and anything making an aggressive move toward you. Cacti are pretty much the same. They have an elaborate defense system that allows them to always be on guard and to always be prepared to fend off invaders. This system also reduces water loss caused by direct sunlight and drying winds.

In this lab, we go medieval on you.

Materials

1   Rectangular floral foam post
1   Box of straight pins
1   Flashlight

Procedure

1. Take the rectangular post of floral foam and stick pins into one side of the shape. Leave the other sides untouched.

2. Shine a flashlight directly onto the floral foam, and then move the flashlight upward in an arc so that it is shining on the foam at 45 degrees, and then directly overhead at 90 degrees.

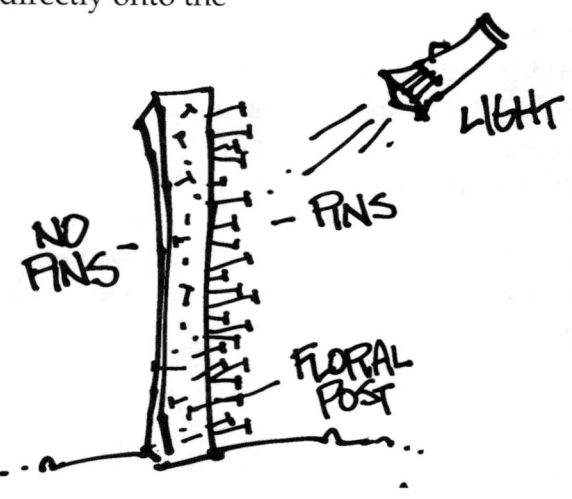

3. At each point in the movement of the flash-light, look at the lengths of the shadows that are cast by the pins that are stuck in the side.

4. Repeat the procedure and draw a picture of the shadows at 0, 45, and 90 degrees overhead.

How Come, Huh?

You should have noticed three things:

A. First of all, no one is going to be very eager to take a bite out of a juicy cactus stem if it means getting a mouthful of stickers. A damaged stem means massive water loss, but a mouthful of stickers means that those that might do the damage will probably avoid the cactus altogether.

B. The needles, narrow as they may be, cast a shadow on the stem as the sun rises higher and higher in the sky. What this means is that, at the hottest part of the day, the needles on the cactus are producing the longest shadows and providing the maximum amount of shading from the sun.

C. Finally, and this was hard to pick up in this lab with casual observation, the needles provide a barrier to the dry, desert winds that blow. The needles inhibit the movement of the winds near the stem, and this also reduces the amount of water loss that is possible.

The needles, or barbs, also serve another purpose: They provide a method of transport for the cactus. I have personal experience with this method of transport. Visiting the Joshua Tree National Monument years ago, I walked through the Teddy Bear Cholla Cactus Garden. Teddy bear cholla cacti reproduce by producing small, round, "fuzzy" (if you think needles can be fuzzy) baby cacti that drop off the mother plant. If you happen to think it would be funny to kick one and watch it fly through the desert, you will quickly find that the barb-like hooks attach themselves to you (and your toes). I suppose, had I been a passing coyote, this would have been slightly more acceptable.

The Desert Sponge

The Experiment

Water is one of the critical elements necessary for survival in any environment, but especially the desert. In this lab, you are going to take a peek at the characteristics of animals that need to store water but also want to prevent water loss.

Materials

1   Sponge, 3 inches by 3 inches, per person
1   Triple beam balance
1   100 mL beaker
     Water
     Assorted materials
     Imagination

Procedure

1. You are going to be the proud owner of a new animal—a desert sponge. Desert sponges take on a variety of shapes, sizes, and characteristics. In addition to taking on all of these shapes, they, like all animals on this planet, are engaged in a game of adaptation and survival. In our game, your sponge is going to compete against sponges that are created by your classmates.

2. Objectives: To meet the minimum requirements listed next for body parts, openings, and orifices AND retain the largest volume of water, by weight. The sponges that accomplish these two goals most efficiently will be the winners and will survive to see another day.

In the spirit of competition and nature's own statistics, only the top third of the sponges engaged in the contest will live.

3. Body requirements:

A. The size and shape of the sponge cannot be changed permanently by cutting or gluing in any way. However, it is perfectly permissible to fold, twist, or otherwise mangle your sponge to produce a specific body shape.

B. Your sponge may want to have a covering to prevent water loss. Also, like all living animals, your sponge must have a mouth, which happens to be no smaller than 5 mm in diameter. It must also have a waste port, located at your discretion, that is also no smaller than 5 mm.

C. Your sponge is an odd animal. It has seven legs, and its legs must support the weight of the fully soaked sponge so that air can circulate over and under your sponge. The minimum clearance from the tabletop to the bottom of the sponge must be at least half an inch.

D. Your sponge will be weighed on a triple beam balance at the beginning of the competition. It must be fully prepared at the time of weigh-in. 100 mL of water will be added to your sponge via the mouth opening that you created.

Each contestant is responsible for filling her own sponge. Any water that is lost during the process is not recoverable.

The Desert Sponge

E. When all of the water that can be added has been added, the sponge will be weighed again. The starting time is noted and the sponges are all placed in the window, where they are all exposed to the same amount of sunlight. They will sit there for 24 hours and will then be weighed again. The sponges that retain the most water win.

Data & Observations

Time	Weight Empty	Weight Full	Weight at End

How Come, Huh?

This is a problem that all animals, including humans, deal with constantly. Water is the most important item that we can put into our bodies. It is responsible for regulating our temperature and decomposing foods so that we can get the energy they possess. Water carries away waste products to keep us healthy and free from poisons, and is vital to just about every biochemical process that our bodies perform. The animals that can find, store, and retain the water they need will survive.

Protective Coloration

The Experiment

This experiment is a great excuse to spend the day outside, catch some sunbeams in various colors of paper pockets, and record the ensuing temperature changes.

The amount of heat that is reflected or absorbed means the difference between survival and extinction in many climates. This goes for temperature, as well as extreme climates, such as those of deserts and arctic regions. This lab takes a look at color and how color affects the amount of heat an animal or plant will absorb when it is in direct sunlight.

Materials

5   Thermometers
5   Sheets of paper
     White
     Red
     Blue
     Green
     Black
1   Stapler
1   Clock

Procedure

HOT-DOG FOLD

1. Prepare 5 pockets using the colors listed in the *Materials* section above. Fold a piece of construction paper hot-dog length (long and narrow, for you non-elementary types). Staple the bottom and side of each to form a pocket.

2. Put the thermometers into the pockets and take them out into the sun. Record the temperature and start the clock running. Record the temperature of each pocket every minute for 10 minutes.

Protective Coloration

Data & Observations

Heating Colored Pockets

Time	0	1	2	3	4	5	6	7	8	9	10
White											
Red											
Blue											
Green											
Black											

How Come, Huh?

White surfaces reflect white light and, as such, do not increase in temperature very much. Black surfaces absorb radiant light as well as the infrared light that accompanies it on its journey from the sun. The other colors fit in between the black and white.

Science Fair Extensions

29. Take a peek at the seasons and how the seasons affect the colors of the coats of animals and birds, and even the skins of reptiles. Use this information to infer how color and survival match up, even when the temperature changes are not that great.

Temperature Regulator

The Experiment

To explore the skin, Ruffini's endings, and the ability of the body to not only detect temperature but also regulate temperature, we are going to find out how the body cools itself off and warms itself up, and why this is especially helpful in desert climates.

Materials

1 Bottle of rubbing alcohol
1 Cottonball
1 Liquid crystal thermometer strip
1 Cotton glove
1 Hand

Procedure

1. Place the liquid crystal thermometer strip on the back of your hand, and let it sit there for a minute. You will notice that the numbers on the thermometer change as your body temperature changes. Record the temperature of your hand in the first row of the table on the next page.

2. Put a little bit of rubbing alcohol on a cottonball and swipe the alcohol across the back of your hand where you took the reading. Immediately place the liquid crystal thermometer on the spot where you wiped the alcohol, and take another reading. Record that number in the second row of your data table.

Temperature Regulator

3. Place your hand in a cotton glove and run around the house, school, or neighbor's yard for 3 minutes. Work up a good sweat and then immediately come inside and insert the liquid crystal thermometer into the glove. Be sure to place it on the back of your hand in the same place that you took the original reading. Give it 15 seconds to adjust, and then take a reading. Put that reading in the third row of your data table.

4. Finally, remove the glove and examine your hand. Notice if your sweat glands have been working overtime at all and, if so, how much?

Data & Observations

Condition Tested	Temperature
Hand at Rest	
Rubbed with Alcohol	
Hand in Glove	

How Come, Huh?

There are several different ideas working together here. First of all, you need to recognize that your body is not in favor of big temperature swings. It likes to keep things constant, predictable, and in a very narrow range of acceptable temperatures. To achieve this end, your skin is your first line of defense.

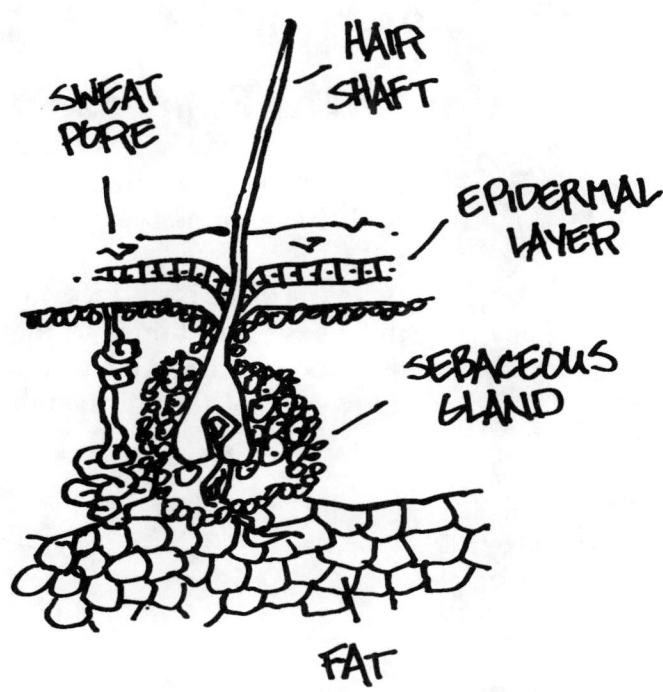

Skin reflects heat, dumps tons of water onto its surface to absorb and displace excess heat, and will even close down the cell openings to the surface in an effort to prevent too much heat gain.

Conversely, the skin also works to prevent too much heat loss. Blue lips in the dead of winter are a sure giveaway that your body has reduced the flow of blood to the skin so that less heat will be lost. Hairs stand on end to trap more air against the body to insulate it from heat loss.

The numbers that you gathered for this lab should have reflected the temperatures generated by three different conditions.

Science Fair Extensions

30. Find out how much heat can be saved by trapping a layer of air next to the body to conserve heat.

Rubber Eggs & Chicken Legs

The Experiment

This activity gives you an opportunity to learn about the kinds of adaptations that birds have made to be able to survive in the wild.

First of all, birds incorporate calcium into their eggs and bones to make them strong, and second, they have a bone design that allows them to be lightweight, and also, to fly.

CHICKEN BONE

VINEGAR

CUP

Materials

4   Fresh chicken wing bones, meat removed
1   16-oz. bottle of distilled, white household vinegar
2   12-oz. plastic cups
1   Fresh egg
1   Spoon

Procedure

1. Remove any remaining meat and cartilage—the soft, whitish-gray matter near the joints—from the chicken bones. Break one of the bones in half and observe the inside. In the interest of good hygiene, you should wash your hands well after picking at these bones.

2. Put the four bones in the first cup and cover them with vinegar. Set them in a place where they will remain undisturbed, as it will take several days for the bones to react completely with the vinegar.

3. Next, put the unbroken fresh egg into the second cup. Pour enough vinegar over the egg to completely cover it. Then, either cover the cup or replace the vinegar as it evaporates. It will take 18 to 24 hours for the egg and vinegar to react completely.

4. After 24 hours, use the spoon to gently remove the egg from the glass. Set it on the table. Carefully push on the egg and observe what used to be the shell. After a few days, remove the wing bones and examine them. Try to bend them and see if they snap as easily as they did when you first started the experiment.

Data & Observations

1. Compare the color and hardness of the chicken bone, both before and after you placed it in the vinegar.

_____

_____

_____

Rubber Eggs & Chicken Legs

2. Compare the color and hardness of the surface of the egg, both before and after you placed it in the vinegar.

_____

_____

_____

How Come, Huh?

Bones and shells are hard because they incorporate a mineral called calcium into their structure. This is why you always see ads telling you to drink your milk and eat your cheese if you want strong bones. Milk and cheese are rich in calcium.

When you placed the bones and the eggs in the vinegar, the vinegar started to attack the calcium and react with it. The calcium was leached, or stolen, from the bones and eggshells. When this happened, the structure of the bones and shells was weakened. It's kind of like taking bricks out of a house. You take enough of them, and the wall gets mooshy. It's the same thing here.

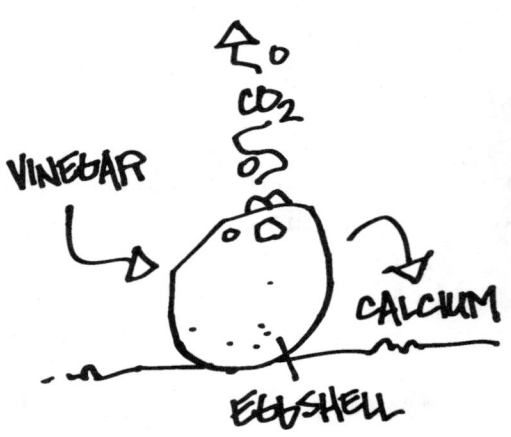

Science Fair Extensions

31. Under the supervision of an adult, you can experiment with other DILUTE acids. Muriatic (hydrochloric) acid is available from pool supply companies, and sulfuric acid can be purchased easily through outlets listed in the Yellow Pages.

Wing Shape

The Experiment

A regular, old, white piece of paper is folded over a pencil, forming the general shape of an airplane wing. As air travels over the top surface of the wing, it creates an area of low pressure and, amazingly enough, demonstrates the principle of lift, which explains why this particular design has been incorporated into bird wings since the beginning of bird wings.

Materials

1   Pencil
1   Paperclip
1   Sheet of paper
1   Pair of scissors
1   Ruler

Procedure

1.   Cut a strip of paper, 3 inches wide by 11 inches long.

2.   Bend the paper in half; do not fold or crease it. Then, clip the two halves of the sheet together, using the paperclip. (You can moosh the paper with your hand so it is flatter, but do not make a crease.)

3.   Slide the pencil into the middle of the paper so that the paperclip hangs down. Hold the "wing" up to your bottom lip and blow down on the top surface of the paper. Use the illustration above as a guide.

If the spirits of Leonardo, Orville, and Wilbur are with you, the wing will be pushed up toward your nose, and you will personally experience Bernoulli's Law in action.

Wing Shape

How Come, Huh?

When you blew across the top of the wing, a difference in air pressure was created. The pressure under the wing remained constant, but the pressure over the wing was reduced. The low pressure on top of the wing allowed the pressure under the wing to push up on it. Aerodynamic engineers call this lift.

The foundation for all of this is Bernoulli's Law, which states that the *faster* a fluid travels *over* the surface of an object, the *less* pressure it puts on that object. Air is considered a fluid, for the purposes of this experiment.

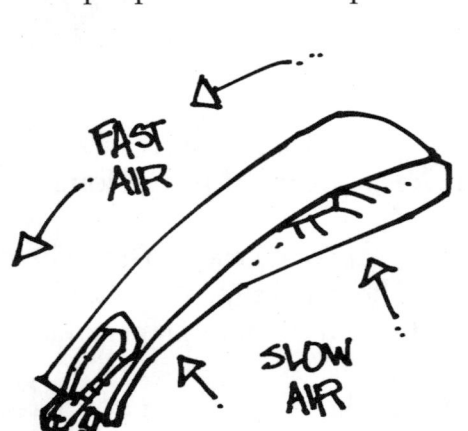

FAST AIR

SLOW AIR

When you think about the experiment, the air under the wing was not moving at all, so the pressure pushing on it remained the same. The air moving across the top of the wing was moving very fast, so it had less time to stop and push on top of the wing. When there is more pressure on the bottom of the wing than on the top, you have lift—illustration at the left.

Science Fair Extensions

32. Experiment with the width and the length of the wing, and prove that regardless of the changes in these two variables, the result is the same.

Ring of Fire

The Experiment

In the previous experiment, we saw the effect of wing shape on movement. In this lab, we are going to be able to see how the convection current moves by watching the behavior of an empty tea bag that has been lit on fire and is burning.

The bag produces a column of hot air, and when the weight of the bag allows it to be lifted up with the rising current of hot air, you have a floating, flammable tea bag. This is one of those labs that you do with an adult around—mostly, because grown-ups get a kick out of this stuff, too.

Materials

1   Tea bag, paper
1   Pie tin
1   Book of matches
    Goggles (optional)
    Adult Supervision

Procedure

DO THIS ACTIVITY OUT-SIDE WHERE THERE IS NO DAN-GER OF CATCHING ANYTHING ON FIRE. You will also want to have an **adult** around to help out.

1. Gently open the top of the tea bag and discard the contents of the bag. Open the tea bag up so that it forms a cylinder, and place it in the center of the pie tin.

2. Under the supervision of an adult, light a match and touch it to the top of the tea bag in several places so that it begins to burn from the top down. Stand back and observe what happens.

Ring of Fire

How Come, Huh?

As the tea bag burned, the air directly above the bag was heated. Hot air rises, so it headed up and out, leaving a vacancy. Cooler air replaced the hot air that rose toward the ceiling, and it, too, was heated by the burning tea bag—off to the ceiling and a convection current was created.

At a certain time in the experiment, the mass of the tea bag had burned down to the point where it could be carried aloft by this current of hot air, and so it lifted off the tin. Because it continued to burn as it floated, it perpetuated the convection current until all of the paper had been consumed. The ash then cooled and fell to the ground. Another mystery of nature is revealed!

Bird wings are adapted for lift. We saw that in the previous lab. If you take that adaptation and show how a convection current is a perfect vehicle for creating lift on that wing, you now understand how birds are able to soar for such long periods of time.

Science Fair Extensions

33. Under adult supervision, experiment with other very light papers, such as wrapping tissue, mimeograph separation sheets, and single-ply toilet paper. If you work it right, they all fly up into the air and produce "oohs" and "aahs" every time.

Big Idea 6

Pollution adversely affects our environment and the ability of plants and animals to live and thrive in their particular ecosystems.

Soapy Seeds

The Experiment

Rachel Carson's book, *Silent Spring*, focused on waterborne pollutants and their effect on living organisms. She endured a firestorm of controversy almost immediately after the release of her book. Her position was eventually proven correct, as a nationwide movement to clean up and preserve our water resources took over, guiding civic groups, legislation, and the American conscience.

This lab demonstrates the effect of a common water pollutant, detergent, on the ability of radish seeds to germinate. It is a valuable lesson for water ecology, and a gentle reminder not to toss your dirty dishwater into the nearby stream the next time you are out camping.

Materials

3   Petri dishes
3   Paper towels
30 Radish seeds
1   1-oz. bottle of
      liquid detergent
1   1 mL pipette
1   Pencil
1   Pair of scissors
    Water

Procedure

1. Place the bottom half of a petri dish on the paper towels, and draw six circles. Cut these discs out, using the scissors. Write "0% Detergent" on the bottom of one paper disc, "1% Detergent" on a second, and "5% Detergent" on a third.

2. Place one of the blank paper discs in a petri dish. Count out 10 radish seeds and space them evenly on the paper disc. Place the "0% Detergent" paper disc on top of these radish seeds. Add 100 drops of water to the paper in the petri dish, and then cover it.

3. Add 99 drops of water and 1 drop of liquid detergent to a second petri dish. Swirl the water and detergent, mixing them thoroughly. Place a blank paper disc into the solution, add 10 radish seeds, evenly spaced, and cover with the paper disc that says "1% Detergent." Cover with the top of the petri dish.

4. Finally, add 95 drops of water and 5 drops of detergent to a third petri dish. Swirl the water and detergent to mix them thoroughly. Place a blank paper disc in the solution, add 10 radish seeds, evenly spaced, and cover with the paper disc that says "5% Detergent." Cover with the top of the petri dish.

5. Set all three petri dishes aside and let them germinate for the entire week. Record your original observations in the leftmost circle on the next page. Check your seeds each day. Draw your observation at the end of the week, 5 days later, in the right circle. Record the number of radish seeds that germinate and grow in the blanks provided near each of the circles.

Soapy Seeds

Data & Observations

DAY 1

DAY 5

Date: _____
Water

Date: _____
Water

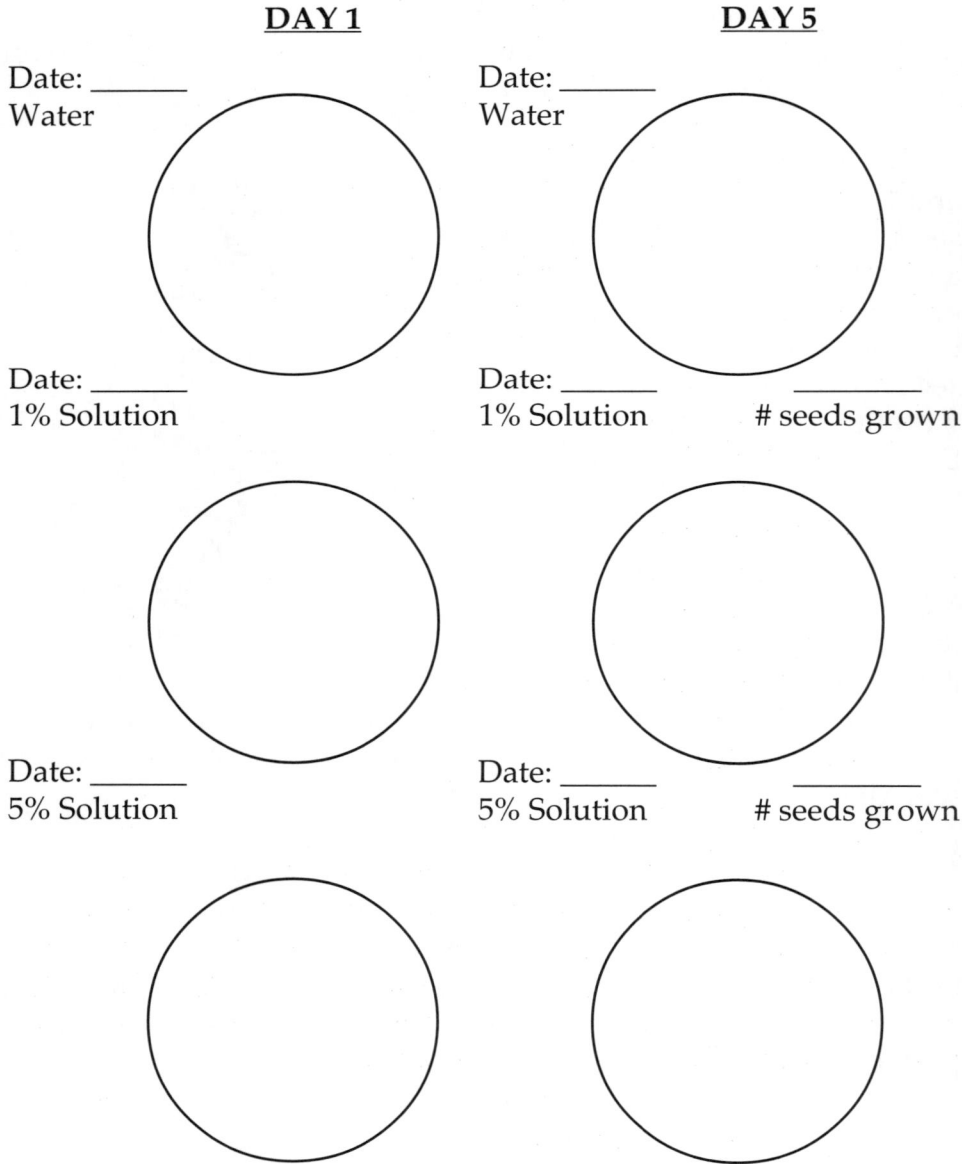

Date: _____
1% Solution

Date: _____
1% Solution

_____
seeds grown

Date: _____
5% Solution

Date: _____
5% Solution

_____
seeds grown

Acid Rain

The Experiment

One of the big environmental problems facing the Eastern United States and much of Europe is acid rain. The big factories and automobiles belch out gases that go into the air, and when mixed with rain, produce acidic solutions. One consequence of this is that marble, which is made out of calcite (calcium carbonate), reacts with dilute acid. In other words, it dissolves. If the problem goes unchecked, we will have statues that look like they are slowly melting as the years pass. This lab will demonstrate the effect of dilute acid on marble.

Materials

1   Drinking glass, 8 oz.
1   Bottle of distilled white vinegar
1   Sample of marble
1   Hand lens or magnifier

Procedure

1. Place the piece of marble in the glass. Fill the glass with vinegar to a level that is one inch above the top of the marble.

2. After a minute or two, examine the marble with the hand lens. You should see small bubbles. This is carbon dioxide gas, being produced on the surface of the rock. Vinegar is a very weak acid. When it comes in contact with the calcium carbonate in the marble, it reacts to produce the gas. A very fine sediment is also produced as a by-product of the reaction. If you let the reaction continue, the marble will dissolve completely.

VINEGAR

MARBLE

Acid Rain

3. To save your marble from eventual disintegration, remove it from the glass and rinse it with water. The alternative, of course, is to let the reaction run its course, in which case, you can say "adios" to your marble.

How Come, Huh?

Marble is formed when limestone or dolomite is heated and squished in the traditional, metamorphic rock manner. Just as quartzite forms when "clean" sandstone is metamorphosed, marble forms from pure limestone or dolomite. Limestone is basically a rock made of calcite (calcium carbonate), and the rock dolomite is made out of the mineral dolomite (magnesium carbonate). With only one mineral present in either of these rocks, new minerals are not formed when metamorphosis starts. However, as is the case with quartzite, the calcite and dolomite recrystallize, grow larger, and fill in any holes in the original rock. The difference is that both calcite and dolomite recrystallize quickly and easily, which gives marble very large crystal grains. Also, the chemical bonds in marble are quite weak when compared to those of most other minerals. As a result, marble breaks, bends, and folds very easily compared to other rocks during the process of metamorphosis. You could say that marble is the Silly Putty of the rock world.

Water Hardness

The Experiment

Different areas of the country have different kinds of water. This is due in large part to the source of the water, what kind of aquifer the supply is being pulled from, or if there is any open air while the water is in transit. All of these things affect the hardness and quality of the water that we drink, cook with, and use for cleaning. This activity lets you test water for hardness, which is determined by the amount of mineral matter dissolved in it. The more mineral matter in the water, the harder the water.

To measure water's hardness, you will test the ability of the water to foam, when detergent is added. Typically, hard water does not foam easily and requires additional detergent to clean clothes and dishes.

Materials

1   1-oz. bottle of liquid detergent
3   16 mm x 150 mm test tubes
1   1 mL plastic pipette
1   1-oz. bottle of calcium acetate powder
1   Spoon
    Distilled water, 4 oz.
    Tap water

Procedure

1. Using the distilled water, fill one test tube 1/4-full. Using the pipette, add a large drop of liquid detergent to the same test tube. Place your thumb over the end of the tube and shake it vigorously. Record your observations by drawing what you see on a separate sheet of paper. Label your drawing, "soft water."

Water Hardness

2. Time to make some hard water. Fill the second test tube 1/4-full with distilled water. Add 1/2-spoonful of calcium acetate powder to the same test tube. Place your thumb over the top and shake the tube for 15 seconds to dissolve as much of the chemical as you can. If there is a little bit left at the bottom the tube, don't worry. As the chemical dissolves, it creates the same effect as hard water. There are all sorts of "minerals" floating around in the water. That's what makes it hard.

3. Using the pipette, add one big drop of liquid detergent to the "hard water" test tube. Place your thumb over the end and shake the tube well. Record your observations by drawing what you see on a separate sheet of paper, labeled "hard water."

4. This time, fill the third test tube with a sample from the tap. Use the same amount of water that you did in the first two tests. Add one drop of liquid detergent, put your thumb over the end, shake, and observe. Draw what you see on a sheet that you label, "tap water." Determine if the tap water is hard or soft by looking at the amount of foam at the top of the tube.

How Come, Huh?

Water hardness affects the taste of the water and how well it performs in cleaning clothes and dishes. There can also be long-term health effects if you drink hard water. There are both good and bad effects.

Ozone Layer

The Experiment

Way up in our atmosphere, there is a layer of ozone. This particular chemical has been in the news for a number of years. The reason that we are concerned about it is that ozone is responsible for protecting our planet from excessive UV rays. These rays damage surfaces, cause skin cancer, and create havoc with most organic things. We are in the process of depleting the ozone layer with the pollution that we are creating.

When light strikes an object, it can be completely reflected, absorbed, diffused, or transmitted. The terms used to describe images based on the way light affects them are *opaque, translucent,* and *transparent.* They are the focus of this lab, which will give you an idea of why it is so difficult to see the surface of Venus from Earth, using a conventional telescope.

Materials

1   Sheet of wax paper
1   Sheet of clear plastic wrap
1   Pair of scissors
2   Rubberbands
2   Toilet paper tubes
1   Flashlight

COVERING

RUBBER-BAND

TOILET PAPER TUBE

Procedure

1. Cut the sheet of wax paper and the sheet of clear plastic wrap in half.

2. Take one of the halves of plastic wrap and wrap it around the end of one of the toilet paper tubes. Secure it with one of the rubberbands. Do the same thing with the other toilet paper tube and the other piece of plastic wrap, so that you have a matched set.

Ozone Layer

3. Hold the tubes up to your eyes and attempt to look around the room. Record your observations in the *Data & Observations* section on this page.

4. Repeat the procedure, making and using a set of wax paper binoculars. Record your observations below.

5. Set one of each tube—plastic wrap and wax paper—on a table that is about 5 feet away from you. Dim the lights so that the room is as dark as you can get it, and shine a flashlight on the two surfaces attached to the toilet paper tubes. Compare the amount of light that is reflected from the plastic wrap to the amount of light that is reflected from the wax paper.

Data & Observations

1. Type of image seen when looking around the room with:

A. Plastic Wrap: _____

_____

B. Wax Paper: _____

_____

2. Type of reflection seen when looking at the reflected surfaces of:

A. Plastic Wrap: _____

_____

B. Wax Paper: _____

_____

How Come, Huh?

The wax paper reflects some of the light that strikes it, and allows some of it to pass through. This produces a fuzzy image that is described as *translucent*. This is why the ozone layer is so important to the survival and health of the planet. The ozone is like the wax paper. It reflects some of the harmful UV rays back out into space.

If we persist in producing chemicals that are dumped into the atmosphere and that go up and destroy the ozone, we may be signing our own eviction notice.

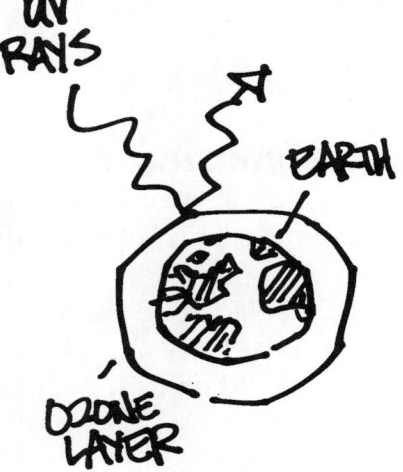

Greenhouse Effect

The Experiment

Scientists have discovered that the atmosphere of Venus is 96% carbon dioxide, which creates surface temperatures of almost 900 degrees Fahrenheit. If that little tidbit of trivia simply slid in one ear and out the other, we would like to run it through the gauntlet again, with a little bit of neural Velcro this time. 900 degrees Fahrenheit. Why? That's the point of this lab.

Materials

2   Quart jars with lids
1   Sheet of wax paper
3   Thermometers
1   Clock with second hand
1   Sun or lamp

Procedure

1.   Find a nice, sunny location or, if the weather is being uncooperative, find a high-powered lamp.

2.   Place one thermometer on a flat surface, with sunlight shining on it. Place a second thermometer inside one of the quart jars and put the lid on it.

3.   Line the third jar with wax paper, insert a thermometer, and put the lid on the jar. Then, line all three thermometers up.

4.   In the *Data & Observations* section, record the temperature readings for each of the three thermometers, every five minutes for one hour. Use that data to draw conclusions about why the atmospheres of the Earth and Venus are so different and, in particular, why the surface temperatures of both planets are so different.

Data & Observations

Time	Bare Thermometer	Clear Jar	Wax Jar
0			
5			
10			
15			
20			
25			
30			
35			
40			
45			
50			
55			
60			

Greenhouse Effect

How Come, Huh?

When you look at the three temperatures, you are looking at models for Mercury (bare thermometer), which has almost no atmosphere, Venus (wax jar), which has a heavy, dense carbon dioxide atmosphere, and Earth (clear jar), which has an atmosphere, but one that is much thinner than that of Venus.

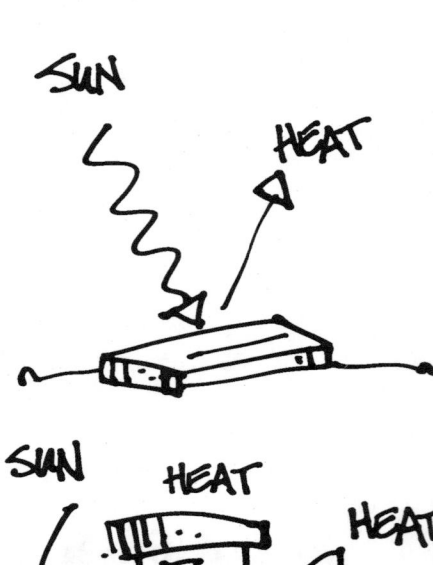

With the first model, there is nothing to prevent the heat from striking the surface of the planet and then radiating back into space. With Venus, the cloud layer over the planet is so thick and dense that any heat that penetrates that cloud layer bounces off the surface and then is reflected again by the cloud layer. This is why Venus is the hottest planet in the solar system.

Earth also has a cloud layer, but it is not thick and persistent. So, whereas heat is absorbed by the planet, much of it is re-radiated back into space. That is why clear, starry nights are so much colder than overcast nights. The cloud layer acts like a big blanket over the Earth.

Science Fair Extensions

34. Venus is only one of two planets with a backward rotation. (The other is Pluto.) Find out how this affects the length of the day, the atmosphere, and the speed at which the atmosphere travels over the surface of a planet.

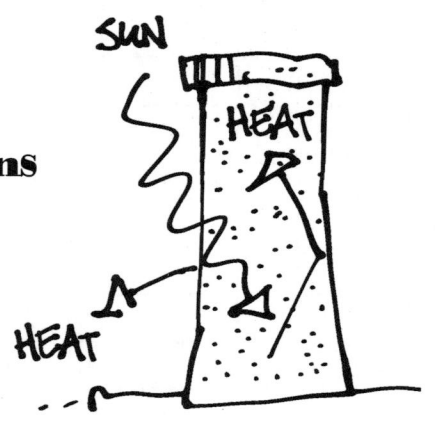

Distilling Fossil Fuels

The Experiment

Coal is an extremely important commodity. It is not only a source of heat and energy, but it also allows us to produce plastics, pesticides, medicines, lubricants, and a host of other goods. Of all the fossil energy sources currently used in North America, coal is the most likely to last for the long term—several centuries, by some estimates.

Because of the various uses that we have for coal, it will be an economically important geological resource for generations to come. You are going to heat a small piece of coal and observe firsthand a couple of its by-products.

Materials

1   Small chip of bituminous coal
        (the size of a pea)
1   Pyrex test tube
1   Test tube holder (clamp)
1   Propane torch
1   Disposable pie tin
1   Pair of goggles
1   Sample of bituminous coal
1   Sample of anthracite coal
1   Sample of lignite coal
    Adult Supervision

Procedure

1. Goggles on and adult supervision! Place the coal chip in the test tube and pick up the tube with the holder. Hold the bottom of the tube over the heat source for a few minutes.

Distilling Fossil Fuels

Technique Time: Hold the tube just over the top of the flame, rather than in the flame. This region is the hottest part of the flame and will not deposit soot on the outside of the tube. Hold the test tube at an angle, so the mouth is not over the flame. The gas that is produced is flammable and, even though the quantity generated is small, it is startling to have a second flame pop up. Holding the test tube at an angle will also keep the walls of the tube cooler, which will aid in the collecting of the liquid portion and will also keep the clamp from overheating.

2.   As the piece of coal heats, you will notice a thick, oily odor caused by heating the coal. Also pay attention to the piece of coal. You may be able to see vapor and liquid bubbling from the fragment. The escaping gas is called **coal gas**, and was used during the 1800s to light street lamps and lamps in city houses.

3.   The brown, oily material on the test tube walls is **coal tar**. Coal tar contains different substances that can be separated for use in the chemical industry. It is used in the production of many organic compounds, including dyes, plastics, synthetic textiles, pesticides, medicines, and much more. Researchers are also looking for ways to use it as a petroleum (oil) substitute.

4.   The solid left over on the bottom of the tube is called **coke** (not to be confused with the soda pop of the same name). Heating bituminous coal drives off compounds, called volatile compounds, that vaporize easily and leave behind a purer form of carbon. Because of its greater purity, it releases more heat when burned than "raw" coal of similar weight. Metallurgy, the purifying and shaping of metal, still uses a great deal of coke.

Data & Observations

Draw a picture of the coal being heated, and label and identify the following: *coal gas*, *coal tar*, and *coke*. Then list the possible uses of each by-product.

Distilling Fossil Fuels

How Come, Huh?

Throughout millions of years of Earth's history, the interiors of continents have occasionally been covered by warm, shallow seas. During these periods, vast areas were covered by swamps, much like today's Everglades or the bayous of the lower Mississippi. Shrubs, ferns, and various types of trees covered hundreds of square miles. When these plants died, they fell into the water but decayed only partially. Warm, stagnant water does not hold oxygen very well, but plant tissue needs oxygen in order to rot completely. As a result, layers and layers of plant material accumulated in the water much faster than the material could decay. This went on over millions of years, resulting in the piling up of literally tons and tons of dead plant matter.

As the plates of the Earth continued to move, changes in sea levels resulted in the burial of these layers under thick sediment. As the amount of sediment increased, the pressure and temperature also increased, cooking the plant matter slowly to form coal. (By the way, if you find this recipe in your family cookbook, be assured that it is very old.) Anyway, during this final step, water and gases were squished out along with mud and sand, leaving nearly pure carbon.

Rock Profile: Coal

How Was It Formed?

True coal comes in two forms, **bituminous** and **anthracite**. Anthracite is simply bituminous coal that has been exposed to greater heat and pressure and is found in areas that have been subjected to intense mountain-building forces. This kind of coal is purer in quality and burns hotter. Bituminous coal is by far the more abundant. It is easy to identify because of its clearly layered appearance and because it is easy to split. Peat is simply plant material that has accumulated in a bog or swamp and has barely changed from its original form. Lignite has undergone somewhat more compaction, and can be thought of as a substance that is halfway between coal and peat.

What's It Used For?

Coal is used to generate electricity, and is also heated to form various materials, such as coal tar, which is used widely in the chemical industry. Nearly all dyes and even medicines, such as aspirin, come indirectly from coal.

Coal has also contributed to the naming of at least one species of dog. A "collier" is a person who works with or sells coal, and a "collie" is a dog. For those people familiar with dogs, they may know that border collies are almost completely black, just like colliers are after a hard day's work.

Where Can I Find It?

Coal can be found in the upper Midwest (Ohio, West Virginia, Pennsylvania, Kentucky, Illinois, Indiana, and Tennessee) and in the central Rocky Mountain states (Utah, Colorado, Montana, and Wyoming).

Science Fair Extensions

35. Determine the heat value of different kinds of coal. If you have access to a bomb calorimeter, using it would be one way to calculate the amount of heat energy stored. If one is not available, there are a couple of other ways available to folks who stick their noses into books and do some research.

DisintegratingStyrofoam

The Experiment

A styrofoam cup is going to be placed in an aluminum tart pan. A small quantity of clear liquid is poured into the cup, and the cup disappears … almost. Amazing and true.

Materials

1   5-inch tart pan
1   6-oz. polystyrene coffee cup
1   Set of fingers
1   Bottle of acetone

Procedure

1.   Gently place the cup upright in the center of the tart pan.

2.   Pour about half an ounce of acetone into the cup and observe what happens. Look for bubbles of gas and the sound of fizzing near the base of the coffee cup.

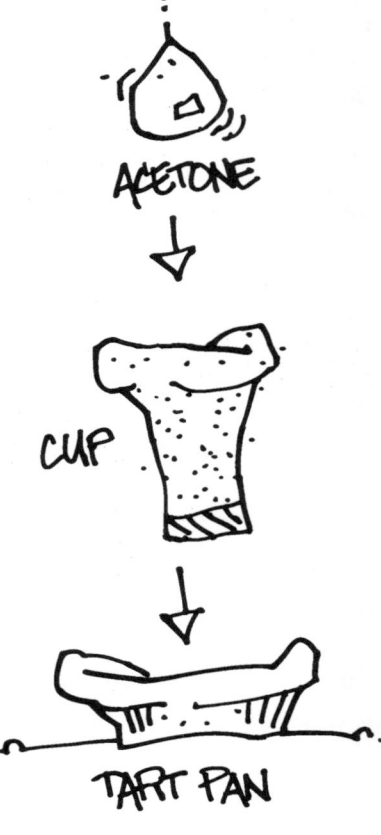

3.   When the cup appears to be completely "dissolved" (our apologies to the chemists of the world), pull the blob out and play with it. The acetone won't hurt your hands, but it may dry out your skin a little bit. In fact, if you look at your skin after you have touched the acetone, you will notice a faint, whitish residue. That's fat from the subcutaneous layer of your skin. Don't get smart and think that you can lose a lot of weight by sitting in a tub of acetone. It only affects the fat that it can get to easily, just under your skin.

4. When you are done, you can either toss the plastic into the recycling bin or let it dry, color it, and give it to your mom as a present.

How Come, Huh?

As soon as the acetone hits the cup, it begins to coagulate, or dissolve, the polystyrene. The acetone is chemically squishing the air out of the spaces in the plastic and, in no time, the cup becomes a blob of styrene.

First of all, let's pick apart this "styrofoam" word. "Styro" is short for a type of plastic called styrene, which is used extensively in the manufacturing of plastics, because it is easy to combine with other molecules. The word "foam" suggests that we have another colloid— a "plastic foam" that was created when a gas (air) was dispersed into a solid (polystyrene).

If we look at the process of creating styrofoam, we find this is true. As the polystyrene was being molded to form the cup, gas was injected into the mixture of plastic and was then trapped in the spaces as it cooled. This trapped air is what allows polystyrene to insulate so well. The acetone causes the polystyrene molecules to unhook from one another, and they just collapse.

OH, NOOOO, NOT ACETONE...

Science Fair Extensions

36. This reaction is the same for all kinds of styrofoam. Take a gallon jar, fill it with a quart of acetone (available from the local hardware store for a couple of bucks), and start adding styrofoam peanuts. You will be able to add several thousand before the container gets even slightly full.

Recycling Plastic

The Experiment

We are going to whip a little recycling information on you, so you can be a little better informed about how to get rid of all the polymers piling up in our environment. In fact, it's our hope that you may be so inspired that you and a couple of your friends might even want to start a recycling program in your school, based on what you are learning. All of the information we present in this lab came from the book, *Hands-on Plastics: A Scientific Investigation Kit*. This book is the result of a joint project between the American Plastics Council and the National Middle Level Science Teachers' Association.

Materials

Variety of plastics

Procedure

1. Head out the door and start collecting different kinds of plastic containers. On the page at the right are the symbols for the six different kinds of plastics that are most commonly manufactured, along with their polymer structures. These symbols are printed somewhere on all plastic containers.

2. Here are the descriptions:
    A. **PETE** Plastic soft drink bottles, mouthwash bottles, peanut butter and salad dressing containers
    B. **HDPE** Milk, water, and juice containers, grocery bags, toys, and liquid detergent bottles
    C. **V** Good, clear packaging and shampoo bottles
    D. **LDPE** Bread bags, frozen food bags, and grocery bags
    E. **PP** Ketchup bottles, yogurt containers, margarine tubs, and medicine bottles
    F. **PS** Video cases, compact disc jackets, coffee cups, meat trays, and fast food sandwich containers

How Come, Huh?

PETE

Polyethylene Terephthalate

HDPE

High Density Polyethylene

V

Polyvinyl Chloride

LDPE

Low Density Polyethylene

PP

Polypropylene

PS

Polystyrene

In 1988, the Society of the Plastics Industry introduced the resin identification coding system for recyclers. This is simply a method of identifying and classifying plastics by the resins that are used to produce them, so that they can be recycled quickly and efficiently.

We have depicted the recycling symbols at the left, along with the "mer," or unit that makes up the polymers.

If you are interested in starting a comprehensive recycling program in your school, you will need bins for all six kinds of resins. Each bin should depict the proper symbol, and kids will need to be educated on how to check for the symbols before they add items to the bins.

Science Fair Projects
•
A Step-by-Step Guide: From Idea To Presentation

Science Fair Projects

Ah, the impending science fair project—a good science fair project has the following five characteristics:

1. The student must come up with an *original* question.
2. That *original* question must be suited to an experiment in order to provide an answer.
3. The *original* idea is outlined with just one variable isolated.
4. The *original* experiment is performed and documented using the scientific method.
5. A presentation of the *original* idea in the form of a lab write-up and display board is completed.

Science Fair Projects

As simple as science report versus science fair project sounds, it gets screwed up millions of times a year by sweet, unsuspecting students who are counseled by sweet, unknowing, and probably just-as-confused parents.

To give you a sense of contrast, we have provided a list of legitimate science fair projects and then reports that do not qualify. We will also add some comments in italics that should help clarify why they do or do not qualify in the science fair project department.

Science Fair Projects

1. Temperature and the amount of time it takes mealworms to change to beetles.

Great start. We have chosen a single variable that is easy to measure: temperature. From this point forward, the student can read, explore, and formulate an original question that is the foundation for the project.

A colleague of mine actually did a similar type of experiment for his master's degree. His topic: The rate of development of fly larvae in cow poop as a function of temperature. No kidding. He found out that the warmer the temperature of the poop, the faster the larvae developed into flies.

2. The effect of different concentrations of soapy water on seed germination.

Again, wonderful. Measuring the concentration of soapy water. This leads naturally into original questions and a good project.

3. Crystal size and the amount of sugar in the solution.

This could lead into other factors, such as exploring the temperature of the solution, the size of the solution container, and other variables that may affect crystal growth. Opens a lot of doors.

vs. Science Reports

4. Helicopter rotor size and the speed at which the 'copter falls.

Size also means surface area, which is very easy to measure. The student who did this not only found the mathematical threshold with relationship to air friction, but she also had a ton of fun.

5. The ideal ratio of baking soda to vinegar to make a fire extinguisher.

Another great start. Easy to measure and track, and leads to a logical question that can either be supported or refuted with the data.

Each of these topics *measures* one thing, such as the amount of sugar, the concentration of soapy water, or the ideal size. If you start with an idea that allows you to measure something, then you can change it, ask questions, explore, and ultimately make a *prediction*, also called a *hypothesis*, and experiment to find out if you are correct. On the other hand, here are some well-meaning but misguided entries:

Science Reports, <u>not Projects</u>
1. Dinosaurs!

OK, great. Everyone loves dinosaurs, but where is the experiment? Did you find a new dinosaur? Is Jurassic Park alive and well, and are we headed there to breed, drug, or in some way test them? Probably not. This was a report on T. rex. Cool, but not a science fair project. And judging by the protest that this kid's mom put up when the kid didn't get his usual "A," it is a safe bet that she put a lot of time in and shared in the disappointment.

More Reports &

2. Our Friend the Sun

Another very large topic, no pun intended. This could be a great topic. Sunlight is fascinating. It can be split, polarized, reflected, refracted, measured, collected, and converted. However, this poor kid simply chose to write about the size of the sun, regurgitating facts about its features, cycles, and other astrofacts while simultaneously offending the American Melanoma Survivors Society. Just kidding about that last part.

3. Smokers' Poll

A lot of folks think that they are headed in the right direction here. Again, it depends on how the kid attacks the idea. Are they going to single out race? Heredity? Shoe size? What exactly are they after here? The young lady who did this report chose to make it more of a psychology-studies effort than a science project. She wanted to know family income, if smokers fought with their parents, how much stress was on the job, and so on. All legitimate concerns, but not placed in the right slot.

4. The Majestic Moose

If you went out and caught the moose, drugged it to see the side effects for disease control, or even mated it with an elk to determine if you could create an animal that would become the spokesanimal for the Alabama Dairy Farmers' Got Melk? promotion, that would be fine. But, another fact-filled report should be filed with the English teacher.

5. How Tadpoles Change into Frogs

Great start, but they forgot to finish the statement. We know how tadpoles change into frogs. What we don't know is how tadpoles change into frogs if they are in an altered environment, if they are hatched out of cycle, or if they are stuck under the tire of an off-road vehicle, blatantly driving through a protected wetland area. That's what we want to know—how tadpoles change into frogs, if, when, or under what measurable circumstances.

Now that we have beaten the chicken squat out of this introduction, we are going to show you how to pick a topic that can be adapted to become a successful science fair project after one more thought.

One Final Comment

A Gentle Reminder

Quite often, I discuss the scientific method with moms, dads, teachers, and kids, and get the impression that, according to their understanding, there is one, and only one, scientific method. This is not necessarily true. There are lots of ways to investigate the world we live in and on.

Paleontologists dig up dead animals and plants but have no way to conduct experiments on them. They're dead. Albert Einstein, the most famous scientist of the last century and probably on everybody's starting five of all time, never did experiments. He was a theoretical physicist, which means that he came up with a hypothesis, skipped over collecting materials for things like black holes and space-time continuums, and didn't experiment on anything or even collect data. He just went straight from hypothesis to conclusion, and he's still considered part of the scientific community. You'll probably follow the six steps we outline, but keep an open mind.

HEY! GOOD NEWS, AL, YOU'RE STILL IN THE CLUB.

Project Planner

This outline is designed to give you a specific timeline to follow as you develop your science fair project. Most teachers will give you 8 to 11 weeks notice for this kind of assignment. We are going to operate from the shorter timeline with our suggested schedule, which means that the first thing you need to do is get a calendar.

A. The suggested time to be devoted to each item is listed in parentheses next to that item. Enter the date of the Science Fair and then, using the calendar, work backward, entering dates.

B. As you complete each item, enter the date that you completed it in the column between the goal (due date) and project item.

Goal   Completed   Project Item

1. Generate a Hypothesis (2 weeks)

_____   _____   Review Idea Section, pp. 166–167
_____   _____   Try Several Experiments
_____   _____   Hypothesis Generated
_____   _____   Finished Hypothesis Submitted
_____   _____   Hypothesis Approved

2. Gather Background Information (1 week)

_____   _____   Concepts/Discoveries Written Up
_____   _____   Vocabulary/Glossary Completed
_____   _____   Famous Scientists in Field

& Timeline

Goal   *Completed*   *Project Item*

3. Design an Experiment (1 week)

_____	_____	Procedure Written
_____	_____	Lab Safety Review Completed
_____	_____	Procedure Approved
_____	_____	Data Tables Prepared
_____	_____	Materials List Completed
_____	_____	Materials Acquired

4. Perform the Experiment (2 weeks)

_____	_____	Scheduled Lab Time

5. Collect and Record Experimental Data (part of 4)

_____	_____	Data Tables Completed
_____	_____	Graphs Completed
_____	_____	Other Data Collected and Prepared

6. Present Your Findings (2 weeks)

_____	_____	Rough Draft of Paper Completed
_____	_____	Proofreading Completed
_____	_____	Final Report Completed
_____	_____	Display Completed
_____	_____	Oral Report Outlined on Index Cards
_____	_____	Practice Presentation of Oral Report
_____	_____	Oral Report Presentation
_____	_____	Science Fair Setup
_____	_____	Show Time!

Scientific Method
• Step 1 •
The Hypothesis

The Hypothesis

A hypothesis is an edu-cated guess. It is a statement of what you think will probably happen. It is also the most im-portant part of your science fair project because it directs the en-tire process. It determines what you study, the materials you will need, and how the experiment will be designed, carried out, and evaluated. Needless to say, you need to put some thought into this part.

There are four steps to generating a hypothesis:

Step One • Pick a Topic
This should be something that you are interested in study-ing. We would like to politely recommend that you take a peek at physical science ideas (physics and chemistry) if you are a rookie and this is one of your first shots at a science fair project. These kinds of lab ideas allow you to repeat experiments quickly. There is a lot of data that can be collected, and there is a huge variety to choose from.

If you are having trouble finding an idea, all you have to do is pick up a compilation of science activities (like this one) and start thumbing through it. Go to the local library or head to a bookstore and you will find a wide and ever-changing selection to choose from. Find a topic that interests you and start reading. At some point, an idea will catch your eye, and you will be off to the races.

Pick a Topic ...

We hope you find an idea you like between the covers of this book. But we also realize that 1) there are more ideas about ecology than we have included in this book and 2) other kinds of presentations, or methods of writing labs, may be just what you need to trigger a new idea or put a different spin on things. So, without further ado, we introduce you to several additional titles that may be of help to you in developing a science fair project.

1. *The Big Book of Nature Projects* Written by The Children's School of Science. ISBN 0-500-01773-5. Published by Thames and Hudson, Inc. 128 pages.

Let the exploration of the world begin! This book walks you through the world of nature, on land, sea, and air. It presents experiments that will help you understand the creatures inhabiting the globe, and offers suggestions for field trips to get you out into the world to see it all for yourself.

2. *Ecology for Every Kid* Written by Janice VanCleave. ISBN 0-471-10086-2. Published by John Wiley & Sons, Inc. 219 pages.

Janice VanCleave is popular for her broad spectrum of book topics. This book on ecology presents activities for kids to use in schools, science fairs, and just for fun. From planting tiny seeds to discussing climates in the mountains, this book covers a broad range of information about the exciting world in which we live.

3. *How Nature Works* Written by David Burnie. ISBN 0-89577-391-0. Published by Reader's Digest. 192 pages.

This great big book is stuffed full with facts and experiments that will bring the world of nature out of the wild and into your living room. It presents 100 ways that the whole family can come to better understand the secrets of nature.

Find an Idea You Like

4. *The Everything Kids' Nature Book* Written by Kathiann M. Kowalski. ISBN 1-58062-321-2. Published by Adams Media Corporation. 132 pages.

Undoubtedly, you will love this book, with its unique look at the things you see in your world each day. It is written with young kids in mind, and with experiments like recreating mountains and lessons like how earthquakes tear them down, you won't want to put this book down until after you've gotten to the last page.

5. *The Kids' Nature Book* Written by Susan Milord. ISBN 0-8368-1967-5. Published by Gareth Stevens Publishing. 142 pages.

You'll never be bored again with this book, and because there are 365 activities for indoors and outdoors, there will be a new lesson to learn every day of the year. Both kids and adults alike will enjoy the wide range of experiments and activities within these pages.

6. *Nature In Your Backyard* Written by Susan S. Lang. ISBN 1-56294-451-7. Published by The Millford Press. 47 pages.

For those of you who aren't able to take trips around the world to understand the whole planet, this book is for you! Just take this book out into your backyard, and the world in its entire wonder will stand out. All the questions you ever dreamed up, and many more, will be answered as you read this full-color book.

7. *Play and Find Out about Nature* Written by Janice VanCleave. ISBN 0-471-12939-9. Published by John Wiley & Sons, Inc. 122 pages.

Janice VanCleave is at it again, with a book that's truly grand in its simple yet informative presentation of the nature of nature. This book will fuel your imagination to search out the secrets of nature, long after you've finished reading it.

Develop an Original Idea

Step Two • Do the Lab

Choose a lab activity that looks interesting, and try the experiment. Some kids make the mistake of thinking that all you have to do is find a lab in a book, repeat the lab, and you are on the gravy train with biscuit wheels. Your goal is to ask an ORIGINAL question, not repeat an experiment that has been done a bazillion times before.

As you do the lab, be thinking not only about the data you are collecting, but of ways you could adapt or change the experiment to find out new information. The point of the science fair project is to have you become an actual scientist and contribute a little bit of new knowledge to the world.

You know that they don't pay all of those engineers good money to sit around and repeat other people's lab work. The company wants new ideas, so if you are able to generate and explore new ideas, you become very valuable, not only to the company but to society. It is the question-askers that find cures for diseases, create new materials, figure out ways to make existing machines energy-efficient, and change the way that we live. For the purpose of illustration, we are going to take a lab titled, "Prisms, Water Prisms," from another book, *Photon U*, and run it through the rest of the process. The lab uses a tub of water, an ordinary mirror, and light to create a prism that splits the light into the spectrum of the rainbow. Cool. Easy to do. Not expensive and open to all kinds of adaptations, including the four that we discuss on the next page.

Step Three • Bend, Fold, Spindle, & Mutilate Your Lab

Once you have picked out an experiment, ask if it is possible to do any of the following things to modify it into an original experiment. You want to try to change the experiment to make it more interesting and to find out one new, small piece of information.

Heat it	Freeze it	Reverse it	Double it
Bend it	Invert it	Poison it	Dehydrate it
Drown it	Stretch it	Fold it	Ignite it
Split it	Irradiate it	Oxidize it	Reduce it
Chill it	Speed it up	Color it	Grease it
Expand it	Substitute it	Remove it	Slow it down

If you take a look at our examples, that's exactly what we did to the main idea. We took the list of 24 different things that you could do to an experiment—not nearly all of them, by the way—and tried a couple of them out on the prism setup.

Double it: Get a second prism and see if you can continue to separate the colors further by lining up a second prism in the rainbow of the first.

Reduce it: Figure out a way to gather up the colors that have been produced and mix them back together to produce white light again.

Reverse it: Experiment with moving the flashlight and paper closer to the mirror and farther away. Draw a picture and be able to predict what happens to the size and clarity of the rainbow image.

Substitute it: You can also create a rainbow on a sunny day using a garden hose with a fine-spray nozzle attached. Set the nozzle adjustment so that a fine mist is produced, and move the mist around in the sunshine until you see the rainbow. This works better if the sun is low in the sky; late afternoon is best.

Hypothesis Worksheet

Step Three (Expanded) • Bend, Fold, Spindle Worksheet

This worksheet will give you an opportunity to work through the process of creating an original idea.

A. Write down the lab idea that you want to mangle.

_____

_____

_____

_____

B. List the possible variables you could change in the lab.

    i. _____

    ii. _____

    iii. _____

    iv. _____

    v. _____

CMON. HE SAID TO STRETCH IT.

C. Take one variable listed in section B and apply one of the 24 changes listed below to it. Write that change down and state your new lab idea in the space below. Do that with three more changes.

Heat it	Freeze it	Reverse it	Double it
Bend it	Invert it	Poison it	Dehydrate it
Drown it	Stretch it	Fold it	Ignite it
Split it	Irradiate it	Oxidize it	Reduce it
Chill it	Speed it up	Color it	Grease it
Expand it	Substitute it	Remove it	Slow it down

    i. _____

_____

_____

_____

ii. _____

_____

_____

_____

iii. _____

_____

_____

_____

iv. _____

STRETCHING!

_____

_____

Step Four • Create an Original Idea — Your Hypothesis
Your hypothesis should be stated as an opinion. You've done the basic experiment, you've made observations, you're not stupid. Put two and two together and make a PREDICTION. Be sure that you are experimenting with just a single variable.

A. State your hypothesis in the space below. List the variable.
i. _____

_____

_____

_____

ii. Variable Tested: _____

Sample Hypothesis Worksheet

On the previous two pages is a worksheet that will help you develop your thoughts and a hypothesis. Here is sample of the finished product to help you understand how to use it.

A. Write down the lab idea that you want to mutilate.
A mirror is placed in a tub of water. A beam of light is focused through the water onto the mirror, producing a rainbow on the wall.

B. List the possible variables you could change in the lab.
    i. **Source of light**
    ii. **The liquid in the tub**
    iii. **The distance from flashlight to mirror**

C. Take one variable listed in section B and apply one of the 24 changes to it. Write that change down and state your new lab idea in the space below.

The shape of the beam of light can be controlled by making and placing cardboard filters over the end of the flashlight. Various shapes, such as circles, squares, and slits will produce different quality rainbows.

D. State your hypothesis in the space below. List the variable. Be sure that when you write the hypothesis, you are stating an idea and not asking a question.

Hypothesis: The narrower the beam of light, the tighter, brighter, and more focused the reflected rainbow will appear.

Variable Tested: The opening on the filter.

Scientific Method
• Step 2 •
Gather Information

Gather Information

Read about your topic and find out what we already know. Check books, videos, the Internet, and movies, talk with experts in the field, and molest an encyclopedia or two. Gather as much information as you can before you begin planning your experiment.

In particular, there are several things that you will want to pay special attention to and that should accompany any good science fair project.

A. Major Scientific Concepts
Be sure that you research and explain the main idea(s) that is / are driving your experiment. It may be a law of physics, a chemical rule, or an explanation of an aspect of plant physiology.

B. Scientific Words
As you use scientific terms in your paper, you should also define them in the margins of the paper or in a glossary at the end of the report. You cannot assume that everyone knows about geothermal energy transmutation in sulfur-loving bacteria. Be prepared to define some new terms for them ... and scrub your hands really well when you are done, if that is your project.

C. Historical Perspective
When did we first learn about this idea, and who is responsible for getting us this far? You need to give a historical perspective with names, dates, countries, awards, and other recognition.

Building a Research Foundation

1. This sheet is designed to help you organize your thoughts and give you some ideas on where to look for information on your topic. When you prepare your lab report, you will want to include the background information outlined below.

    A. *Major Scientific Concepts (Two is plenty.)*

        i. _____

_____

_____

_____

        ii. _____

_____

_____

_____

    B. *Scientific Words (No more than 10)*

        i. _____

        ii. _____

        iii. _____

        iv. _____

        v. _____

        vi. _____

        vii. _____

        viii. _____

        ix. _____

        x. _____

    C. *Historical Perspective*
        Add this as you find it.

2. There are several sources of information that are available to help you fill in the details from the previous page.

A. *Contemporary Print Resources*
   (Magazines, Newspapers, Journals)
   i. _____
   ii. _____
   iii. _____
   iv. _____
   v. _____
   vi. _____

B. *Other Print Resources*
   (Books, Encyclopedias, Dictionaries, Textbooks)
   i. _____
   ii. _____
   iii. _____
   iv. _____
   v. _____
   vi. _____

C. *Celluloid Resources*
   (Films, Filmstrips, Videos)
   i. _____
   ii. _____
   iii. _____
   iv. _____
   v. _____
   vi. _____

D. Electronic Resources
   (Internet Website Addresses, DVDs, MP3s)

      i. _____

     ii. _____

    iii. _____

    iv. _____

     v. _____

    vi. _____

   vii. _____

  viii. _____

    ix. _____

     x. _____

E. Human Resources
   (Scientists, Engineers, Professionals, Professors, Teachers)

      i. _____

     ii. _____

    iii. _____

    iv. _____

     v. _____

    vi. _____

You may want to keep a record of all of your research and add it to the back of the report as an Appendix. Some teachers who are into volume think this is really cool. Others, like myself, find it a pain in the tuchus. No matter what you do, be sure to keep an accurate record of where you find data. If you quote from a report word for word, be sure to give proper credit with either a footnote or parenthetical reference. This is very important for credibility and accuracy. This will keep you out of trouble with plagiarism (copying without giving credit).

Scientific Method
• Step 3 •
Design Your Experiment

Acquire Your Lab Materials

The purpose of this section is to help you plan your experiment. You'll make a map of where you are going, how you want to get there, and what you will take along.

List the materials you will need to complete your experiment in the table below. Be sure to list multiples if you will need more than one item. Many science materials double as household items in their spare time. Check around the house before you buy anything from a science supply company or hardware store. For your convenience, we have listed some suppliers on page 19 of this book.

	Material	Qty.	Source	$
1.				
2.				
3.				
4.				
5.				
6.				
7.				
8.				
9.				
10.				
11.				
12.				

Total $_____

Outline Your Experiment

This sheet is designed to help you outline your experiment. If you need more space, make a copy of this page to finish your outline. When you are done with this sheet, review it with an adult, make any necessary changes, review safety concerns on the next page, prepare your data tables, gather your equipment, and start to experiment.

In the space below, list what you are going to do in the order you are going to do it.

i. _____

_____

_____

_____

ii. _____

_____

_____

_____

iii. _____

_____

_____

_____

iv. _____

_____

_____

_____

v. _____

_____

_____

_____

Evaluate Safety Concerns

We have included an overall safety section in the front of this book on pages 16-18, but there are some very specific questions you need to ask and prepare for, depending on the needs of your experiment. If you find that you need to prepare for any of these safety concerns, place a check mark next to the letter.

_____ *A. Goggles & Eyewash Station*
If you are mixing chemicals or working with materials that might splinter or produce flying objects, goggles and an eyewash station or sink with running water should be available.

_____ *B. Ventilation*
If you are mixing chemicals that could produce fire, smoke, fumes, or obnoxious odors, you will need to use a vented hood or go outside and perform the experiment in the fresh air.

_____ *C. Fire Blanket or Fire Extinguisher*
If you are working with potentially combustible chemicals or electricity, a fire blanket and extinguisher nearby are a must.

_____ *D. Chemical Disposal*
If your experiment produces a poisonous chemical or there are chemical-filled tissues (as in dissected animals), you may need to make arrangements to dispose of the by-products from your lab.

_____ *E. Electricity*
If you are working with materials and developing an idea that uses electricity, make sure that the wires are in good repair, that the electrical demand does not exceed the capacity of the supply, and that your work area is grounded.

_____ *F. Emergency Phone Numbers*
Look up and record the following phone numbers for the Fire Department: _____ , Poison Control: _____ , and Hospital: _____ . Post them in an easy-to-find location.

Prepare Data Tables

Finally, you will want to prepare your data tables and have them ready to go before you start your experiment. Each data table should be easy to understand and easy for you to use.

A good data table has a **title** that describes the information being collected, and it identifies the **variable** and the **unit** being collected on each data line. The variable is *what* you are measuring and the unit is *how* you are measuring it. They are usually written like this:

Variable (unit), or to give you some examples:

Time (seconds)
Distance (meters)
Electricity (volts)

An example of a well-prepared data table looks like the sample below. We've cut the data table into thirds because the book is too small to display the whole line.

Determining the Boiling Point of Compound X_1

Time (min.)	0	1	2	3	4	5	6
Temp. (°C)							

Time (min.)	7	8	9	10	11	12	13
Temp. (°C)							

Time (min.)	14	15	16	17	18	19	20
Temp. (°C)							

Scientific Method
• Step 4 •
Conduct the Experiment

Lab Time

It's time to get going. You've generated a hypothesis, collected the materials, written out the procedure, checked the safety issues, and prepared your data tables. Fire it up. Here's the short list of things to remember as you experiment.

_____ *A. Follow the Procedure and Record Any Changes*

Follow your own directions specifically as you wrote them. If you find the need to change the procedure once you are into the experiment, that's fine; it's part of the process. Be sure to keep detailed records of the changes. When you repeat the experiment a second or third time, follow the new directions exactly.

_____ *B. Observe Safety Rules*

It's easier to complete the lab activity if you are in the lab rather than in the emergency room.

_____ *C. Record Data Immediately*

Collect temperatures, distances, voltages, revolutions, and any other variables, and immediately record them into your data table. Do not think you will be able to remember them and fill everything in after the lab is completed.

_____ *D. Repeat the Experiment Several Times*

The more data that you collect, the better. It will give you a larger database, and your averages will be more meaningful. As you do multiple experiments, be sure to identify each data set by date and time so you can separate them out.

_____ *E. Prepare for Extended Experiments*

Some experiments require days or weeks to complete, particularly those with plants and animals or the growing of crystals. Prepare a safe place for your materials so your experiment can continue undisturbed while you collect the data. Be sure you've allowed enough time for your due date.

Scientific Method
• Step 5 •
Collect and Display Data

Types of Graphs

This section will give you some ideas on how you can display the information you are going to collect as a graph. A graph is simply a picture of the data that you gathered, portrayed in a manner that is quick and easy to reference. There are four kinds of graphs described on the next two pages. If you find you need a leg up in the graphing department, we have a book in the series that will guide you through the process.

Line and Bar Graphs

These are the most common kinds of graphs. The most consistent variable is plotted on the "x," or horizontal, axis, and the more temperamental variable is plotted along the "y," or vertical, axis. Each data point on a line graph is recorded as a dot on the graph, and then all of the dots are connected to form a picture of the data. A bar graph starts on the horizontal axis and moves up to the data line.

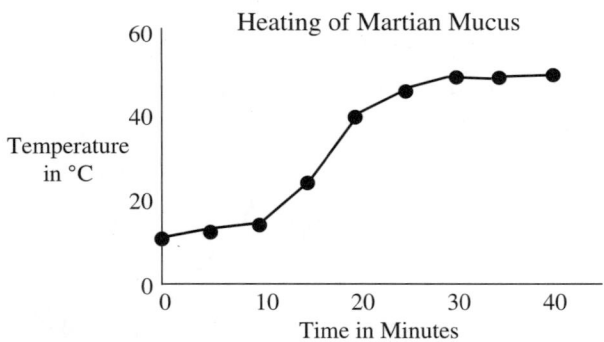

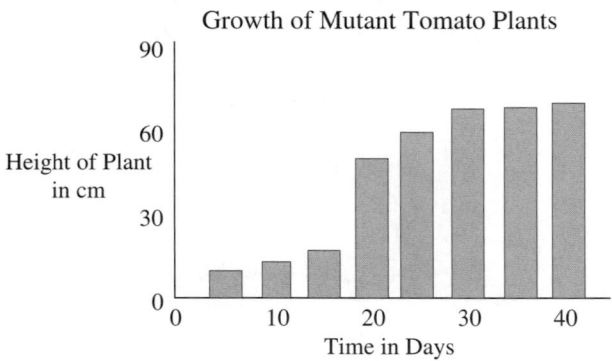

Best Fit Graphs

A best fit graph was created to show averages or trends rather than specific data points. The data that has been collected is plotted on a graph, just as on a line graph, but instead of drawing a line from point to point to point, which sometimes is impossible anyway, you just freehand a line that hits "most of the data."

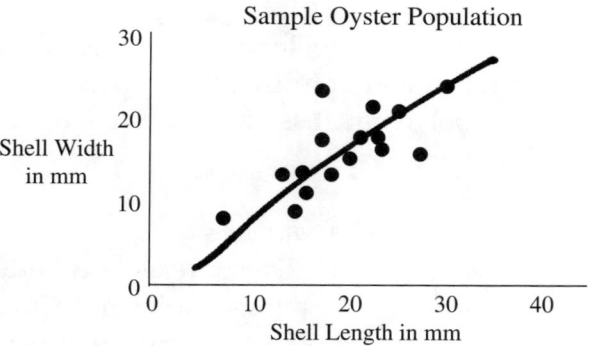

Pie Graphs

Pie graphs are used to show relationships between different groups. All of the data is totaled up, and a percentage is determined for each group. The pie is then divided to show the relationship between one group and another.

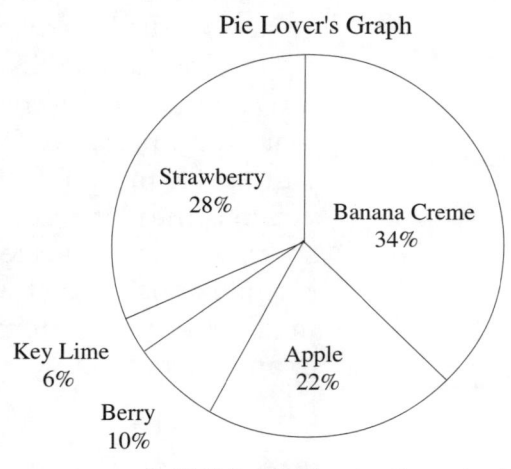

Other Kinds of Data

1. Written Notes & Observations

This is the age-old technique used by all scientists. Record your observations in a lab book. Written notes can be made quickly as the experiment is proceeding, and they can then be expounded upon later. Quite often, notes made in the heat of an experiment are revisited during the evaluation portion of the process, and they can shed valuable light on how or why the experiment went the way it did.

2. Drawings

Quick sketches as well as fully developed drawings can be used as a way to report data for a science experiment. Be sure to title each drawing and, if possible, label what it is that you are looking at. Drawings that are actual size are best.

3. Photographs, Videotapes, and Audiotapes

These are usually better than drawings, quicker to produce, and more accurate, but you do have the added expense and time of developing the film. However, they can often capture images and details that are not usually seen by the naked eye.

4. The Experiment Itself

Some of the best data you can collect and present is the actual experiment, itself. Nothing will speak more effectively for you than the plants you grew, the specimens you collected, or that big pile of tissue that was an armadillo you peeled from the tread of an 18-wheeler.

Scientific Method
· Step 6 ·
Present Your Ideas

Oral Report Checklist

It is entirely possible that you will be asked to make an oral presentation to your classmates. This will give you an opportunity to explain what you did and how you did it. Quite often, this presentation is part of your overall score, so if you do well, it will enhance your chances for one of the bigger awards.

To prepare for your oral report, your science fair presentation should include the following components:

Physical Display

_____a. freestanding display board
    hypothesis
    data tables, graphs, photos, etc.
    abstract (short summary)

_____b. actual lab setup (equipment)

Oral Report

_____a. hypothesis or question
_____b. background information
    concepts
    word definitions
    history or scientists
_____c. experimental procedure
_____d. data collected
    data tables
    graphs
    photos or drawings
_____e. conclusions and findings
_____f. ask for questions

Set the display board up next to you on the table. Transfer the essential information to index cards. Use the index cards for reference, but do not read from them. Speak in a clear voice, hold your head up, and make eye contact with your peers. Ask if there are any questions before you finish and sit down.

Written Report Checklist

Next up is the written report, also called your lab write-up. After you compile or sort the data you have collected during the experiment and evaluate the results, you will be able to come to a conclusion about your hypothesis. Remember, disproving an idea is as valuable as proving it.

This sheet is designed to help you write up your science fair project and present your data in an organized manner. This is a final checklist for you.

To prepare your write-up, your science fair report should include the following components:

_____ a.   binder
_____ b.   cover page, title, & your name
_____ c.   abstract (a one-paragraph summary)
_____ d.   table of contents with page numbers
_____ e.   hypothesis or question
_____ f.   background information
                concepts
                word definitions
                history or scientists
_____ g.   list of materials used
_____ h.   experimental procedure
                written description
                photo or drawing of setup
_____ i.   data collected
                data tables
                graphs
                photos or drawings
_____ j.   conclusions and findings
_____ k.   glossary of terms
_____ l.   references

Display Checklist

Prepare your display to accompany the report. A good display should include the following:

Freestanding Display

_____ a.   freestanding cardboard back

_____ b.   title of experiment

_____ c.   your name

_____ d.   hypothesis

_____ e.   findings of the experiment

_____ f.   photo or illustrations of equipment

_____ g.   data tables or graphs

Additional Display Items

_____ h.   a copy of the write-up

_____ i.   actual lab equipment setup

Glossary & Index

Glossary

Acid rain

When we use coal to produce electricity or gasoline to run our cars, engines emit gases—most notably, carbon dioxide, sulfur dioxide, and carbon monoxide—that rise up into the atmosphere. These gases then become part of the air that we breathe and the clouds that we see. Once they are up in the atmosphere, they act as condensation nuclei, and rain droplets form on these acidic molecules—hence the name, acid rain. The water falls from the sky and changes the pH of the water and soil, eats away at marble buildings and statues, and pollutes the environment.

Adaptation

The ability of a plant or animal to make changes to survive in a particular environment. This may be figuring out how to deal with the excessive heat of the desert, lots of shade, if you are hanging out at the bottom of the rain forest, or extreme cold, if you happen to live in the tundra or arctic regions of the world. These adaptations allow the plants or animals to live, reproduce, and thrive in environments that would be deadly to other species.

Atmosphere

This is comprised of the gases surrounding a planet. In the case of the Earth, the gases are primarily nitrogen and oxygen, and the atmosphere is about 100 miles high. Without an atmosphere, we would get zapped by all kinds of nasty rays and more meteorites than we currently have, and it would be tricky to breathe.

Bug board

A chunk of wood that you throw down on a grassy or wooded area to collect bugs, with the idea being that bugs like dark, stinky places to hide from larger animals that like to make them part of their snack time.

Carbon cycle

Carbon is one of the principal atoms in our world. All organic matter is made of long chains of carbon, plants use it to make food, and we use it to expel gases that we no longer need. It is critical. The carbon cycle begins with a plant absorbing carbon dioxide from the air. The plant makes sugars, which are eaten by animals. The animals convert the carbon in the sugars to other compounds they need. The animals are eaten by other animals and are sometimes expelled as gases, called carbon dioxide, to start the cycle over again.

Ecosystem

A collection of plants and animals that are interdependent. Typically, ecosystems are classified as arctic, tundra, temperate, deciduous forest, grassland, high plain, coniferous forest, desert, and rain forest. Within each of these categories, there are specific kinds of ecosystems. For example, in the southwestern United States, we have the Sonoran, Colorado, Mojave, and Chihuahua Deserts.

Evolution

A theory. We'll let the hard-core Evolutionists and Creationists have at this one.

Field journal

A notebook in which you keep a record of your observations, drawings, and loose specimens when you are out and about, studying in the wilds. Typically, it is a written record of what you see on a particular day, and what those observed were doing on that day.

Filter, pondwater

A great way to use your old nylons. You can use this to take a peek at the old bugs that you are going to catch. It's a great excuse to roll up your pants and go wading.

Glossary

Food chain

The pecking order in an ecosystem. Typically, food chains are anchored by plants, which are the producers. Then, a primary consumer, like a bug, comes along and nibbles on the plant until a bird eats the bug. This is the start of a food chain. This is also known as the "Who Eats Whom?" of the ecosystem.

Greenhouse effect

It's when your tan fades because you are spending too much time inside. No, just kidding. As we dump more and more pollutants, particularly carbon dioxide, into the air, the more and more these gases act like the covering to a greenhouse. They allow light and heat energy in, but they do not let it back out. As a consequence, the Earth is heating up by a fraction of a degree every year.

Leaf rubbings

A picture of a leaf that is produced when you put a sheet of paper over a leaf and rub it with a crayon. The pressure of the leaf against the crayon leaves an impression of the leaf.

Metamorphosis

A term used to describe the changes that typically occur in the life of a bug. Unlike mammals, which pop out of the chute and don't really change in appearance that much, bugs start as little spheres, called eggs. They hatch and form worm-like things, called larvae, and crawl around and eat holes in leaves. Then, as they approach their teen years, they get really shy and retreat to a room, called a cocoon, that they stay in while they change into their adult costumes. The adults then run around, have fun, mate, lay eggs, and next spring, the whole process starts all over again.

Nitrogen cycle

The movement of nitrogen through plants, animals, and back into the environment.

Owl pellet

Contrary to popular belief, this is not owl poop. When an owl eats a bird, small rodent, or small mammal, it typically swallows it whole. This whole animal is practically digested and, when all of the useful materials have been consumed, the owl regurgitates this pellet of matted fur, bone, and anything else that it cannot digest. By dissecting the pellet, you can determine the owl's diet and how far it can spit.

Ozone

The desired destination of a number of hard rock groupies. Also a chemical that is found in our upper atmosphere. It is responsible for deflecting harmful UV rays from the surface of the Earth. Ozone has been slowly diminishing over the Poles for several years now, and this fact is causing some concern among environmentalists.

Plant press

A tool that enables you to press your plants flat, dry them out, and preserve them for later study. Typically, a plant press is made of two sheets of wood, a number of sheets of cardboard, and newspaper to absorb the water as the plants dry.

Pooter

The dumbest name ever given to a scientific tool. It is a jar with two hoses attached to it. One hose goes into your mouth, and the other is used to suck small bugs into a container so that they can be studied, sauteed, and mounted for posterity.

Quadrant survey

A method of systematically studying a small niche in an ecosystem. You divide an area into equal sections and record the number and kinds of plants and animals that you find in each of the squares.

Glossary

Recycling
A program, lifestyle, or Scouting requirement that imparts a sense of responsibility for using the natural resources that we have wisely and then reusing them again, if that is possible.

Rock cycle
Everything on the Earth goes around and around, and rocks are no exception. Molten lava shoots out of the ground and produces igneous rocks. These rocks erode and then stack up on lake bottoms. They are called sedimentary rocks. These rocks are then buried deeper and deeper under the crust of the Earth, and they metamorphose into harder metamorphic rocks. If they get buried too deep, they melt and turn back into lava.

Seasons
Fall, winter, spring, and summer. Created primarily by the tilt of the Earth's axis, relative to the position of the sun.

Spore print
A spore print is created when the cap of a mature mushroom is placed upside down on a sheet of construction paper. The spores, or reproductive organs of the mushroom, are deposited on the surface of the paper in a pattern consistent with their position on the mushroom cap. When the spores have all landed on the paper, they can be secured in place with a spray fixative.

Spreading board
A board made of soft wood that is used to shape, dry, and ultimately prepare winged insect specimens for collection. The insect body is placed in a narrow cavity created by two boards, and the wings are positioned by the collector and held in place with narrow paper strips. Once the insect is dry, it is mounted and catalogued.

Symbiosis

A mutually-beneficial association between two organisms. One of the most common examples is a lichen. A lichen is a marriage between an alga and a fungus. The fungus provides the "house" for the alga to live in, and the alga, having chlorophyll, produces food for the fungus. Both are better off as a result of their association.

Trackway grid

A trackway grid is a tool used by people who study mammals to collect tracks by baiting an area that has been raked smooth with food. The food attracts the animals who leave their prints in pursuit of the food. Scientists can then determine the sizes, genders, and numbers of animals in an area from their trackways.

Transect survey

This is a quadrant survey, rotated 90 degrees. Instead of looking at an area from the top down, you are taking a sideways survey of a plant population. Imagine that you are looking at a wire fence along a country road. You would divide the different areas that you are looking at by the height of the wire running across the survey. A transect survey does the same thing. It sorts plants by their heights.

Water cycle

Probably the most common and well-known of the different cycles, the water cycle starts with the evaporation of water into the sky. There, it forms clouds, which dump their precipitation onto the ground as rain, snow, sleet, hail, or ice. The water melts, collects in creeks, then streams, then rivers, and runs back into oceans.

Index

Index

Notes

Notes

Notes

Notes

The Original World Wide Web • B. K. Hixson

Notes

More Science Books

Thermodynamic Thrills
50 hands-on lab activities that investigate heat via conduction, convection, radiation, specific heat, and temperature.

Dig It!
50 hands-on lab activities that delve into the world of rock and mineral identification. Igneous, sedimentary, and metamorphic rocks, at your rock hammer!

Newton Take 3
50 hands-on lab activities that explore the world of mechanics, forces, gravity, and Newton's three laws of motion.

Le Boom du Jour
50 more hands-on lab activities from the world of chemistry. Learn about polymers, pH, electrochemistry, and occasional rapid oxidation.

50 Science Zingers
50 hands-on lab activities that are collected from all areas of physics and chemistry, presented in a format where you have to figure out what happens and why.

Anatomy Academy
50 hands-on lab activities that delve into the inner workings of the human body. Head to toe, inside to outside, we have you covered.